The Songs of Insects

P9-CLR-484

Oblong-winged Katydid

The Songs of Insects

Handsome Trig

Lang Elliott and Wil Hershberger

with photos and sound recordings
by the authors

Houghton Mifflin Company
Boston   New York
2007

Nebraska Conehead

Copyright © 2006 by Lang Elliott, NatureSound Studio

All rights reserved

No part of this publication may be reproduced, stored, or introduced into a retrieval
system, or likewise copied in any form, without the prior permission of the publisher,
except for review or citation. For more information about permissions to reproduce
selections from this book, write to Permissions, Houghton Mifflin Company, 215
Park Avenue South, New York, New York 10003.

Visit our Web site: www.houghtonmifflinbooks.com

Library of Congress Cataloging-in-Publication Data

Elliott, Lang.
The songs of insects / Lang Elliott and Wil Hershberger;
with photos and sound recordings by the authors.
p. cm.
Includes index.
ISBN-13: 978-0-618-66397-2
ISBN-10: 0-618-66397-5
1. Insect sounds — East (U.S.) — Pictorial works.
2. Sound production by insects — East (U.S.) — Pictorial works.
I. Hershberger, Wil. II. Title.
QL496.5.E45 2006
595.7159 — dc22   2006033294

Book design by Lang Elliott,
NatureSound Studio, P.O. Box 84,
Ithaca, New York 14851-0084

Cover photo: Broad-winged Tree Cricket by Wil Hershberger

Printed in China

C&C 10 9 8 7 6 5 4 3 2 1

Handsome Meadow Katydid

Contents

Black-horned Tree Cricket

Foreword

In 2000, when Lang Elliott told me he was planning a book about singing insects, I was both skeptical and delighted—*skeptical* because Lang had no background in the subject and was having the same difficulty in hearing high-pitched insect songs as I was; *delighted* because I had long hoped to see a book of the sort he was proposing and because he had produced similar works of the highest quality when his subjects were birds and frogs.

My skepticism was soon assuaged by his signing, as coauthor, Wil Hershberger, who had authored a first-rate CD of the songs of crickets and katydids of the Mid-Atlantic States, and by his demonstrating that he had an electronic device that was better than mine for making audible the songs of insects that we could no longer hear. Any remaining skepticism quickly disappeared when he and Wil came to Gainesville and I observed the two working together in the field. Especially memorable was a warm June night in 2001, when the three of us acoustically explored the University of Florida's sixty-acre on-campus Natural Area Teaching Laboratory. Among our

Lesser Pine Katydid

discoveries that evening were multitudes of Lesser Pine Katydids calling in the crowns of towering pine trees. This species had long ago become inaudible to my aging ears, and only the electronics and sensitive microphones of Lang's SongFinder made it possible for me to hear and appreciate the chorus. Our discoveries did not end there. Not far down the trail we homed in on an Eastern Striped Cricket, which Wil and Lang promptly collected for photography, and then Wil's keen ears led us to a Broad-winged Tree Cricket, the first specimen ever to be found this far south.

During the following years, as the two expanded their collection of photographs and song recordings, and I occasionally helped by identifying problem species, it became evident that they had set such high standards for their book that they were repeatedly willing to wait for the next singing season to get the sights and sounds they judged should be included. Thus, when they finally were ready to submit their book to the publisher and sent me the page layouts to review, I was pleased but not surprised to see that they had included the very species I would hope to see in a book of this type. And the portraits and natural shots were gorgeous, fully doing justice to the striking beauty of my favorite animals, the singing insects.

Thomas J. Walker,
founder and Webmaster of
Singing Insects of North America:
www.buzz.ifas.ufl.edu

Linnaeus's 17-year Cicada

Preface

There is a story behind every creation, and this book is no exception. Finger through the pages and you will see beautiful photographs of our native insect songsters, including more than seventy-five crickets, katydids, grasshoppers, and cicadas. Along with photographs of the singers on vegetation, each species is also pictured on white, making it appear as if the insect is standing right on the page. And there is a compact disc in a pouch inside the back cover, containing the songs of all the species recorded. An attractive and useful book, you might think, but how did it come about? What stimulated the creation of this guide?

Perhaps the greatest source of inspiration was a lovely little book by the late Vincent G. Dethier, an entomologist and professor of zoology at the University of Massachusetts. Shortly before his death, Dr. Dethier wrote *Crickets and Katydids, Concerts and Solos.* In it, he celebrates his days as an undergraduate field assistant, collecting insect songsters during the lazy days of summer for George W. Pierce, a physicist who did pioneering work on insect songs in the 1930s and 1940s. Dethier's poetic book portrays the joy of listening to insect songs, and it includes a key to the identification of songs, along with line drawings of some species. After reading Dethier's book, we couldn't help but think how useful it would be to create a practical guide, with photos of every species and with sound recordings of the actual songs.

We are also indebted to Dr. Pierce, not only for his pioneering research, but for providing us with the title for our book. Pierce summarized his research in his classic *Songs of Insects,* published in 1948 by Harvard University Press. Since Pierce's book is long out of print, we decided it would do no harm to use the same title, especially if we brought attention to the original work.

Since we are not trained entomologists or technical experts on insect song, we wondered if we would be able to identify all the songs that we recorded. After doing a little research, we discovered a comprehensive Web site featuring insect songs, the brainchild of Thomas J. Walker, an entomologist at the University of Florida who has devoted much of his professional life to the study of this subject. Tom's Web site, Singing Insects of North America (www.buzz.ifas.ufl.edu), proved absolutely critical to the unfolding of this book.

Last but not least, we want to reveal where we got the idea to photograph insects on a white background. Our source was a delightful little book called *Backyard Bugs,* by Robin Kittrell Laughlin, published in 1996 by Chronicle Books. When we saw Robin's unique photographs, we knew immediately that we should employ her artistic technique in our book. And herein you see the result.

So now you know what stimulated us to create this book and why it looks and sounds the way it does. No idea arises in a vacuum. All creative works depend upon works that precede them, and our book is no exception. In this light, we offer our deepest thanks to Vincent G. Dethier, George W. Pierce, Thomas J. Walker, and Robin Kittrell Laughlin for the inspiration they have provided.

Lang Elliott and Wil Hershberger
August 2006

Introduction

Throughout most of temperate North America, there is a familiar seasonal unfolding of the natural soundscape. Following the eerie quiet of winter, spring erupts with the chorusing of countless frogs and toads, and at dawn we marvel at the excited twittering of the birds, which intensifies as migratory species return in April and May. It is the males that are singing, with the intention of attracting mates or defining breeding territories. The air remains alive with these creatures' sounds through most of June, but thereafter the soundscape mellows as birds and frogs alike complete their breeding cycles and move into other phases of their lives.

Early July seems a time of repose. We may still hear the occasional croak of a frog, and some birds keep singing as if summer will never end, but most species have abandoned their vocal antics and are spending their time raising their young or moving about in family groups. Insect sounds are also sparse. We may notice the chirping of certain early crickets, but the vast majority of insect singers have not yet matured—they are still in nymphal stages, preoccupied with eating, growing, and molting their skins as they march toward adulthood.

But all this changes in midsummer. By late July, the air is filled with the calls of crickets, katydids, and cicadas, and by early August the chorus is overwhelming, with all manner of insects singing both day and night. It is the males who are making the racket, calling to attract females in order to mate. Emily Dickinson's thoughtful stanza from her poem "My Cricket" nicely conveys the onset of the insect chorus. When reading her poem,

be aware that Emily's use of the word "pathetic" is not intended to be derogatory, but rather indicates that the diminutive songsters, invisible in the grass, aroused her heartfelt sympathy and compassion:

> Farther in summer
> Than the birds
> Pathetic from the grass
> A minor nation celebrates
> Its unobtrusive mass
>
> EMILY DICKINSON 1830–1886

This book is an introduction to the songs of seventy-seven crickets, katydids, and cicadas found in eastern and central United States and Canada, east of the Great Plains (many species, however, range more broadly). We have attempted to include nearly all common and widespread species and to provide you with photographs, sound recordings, range maps, and basic natural history information describing each. The cacophony of insect sounds of late summer and early autumn is truly a challenge to decipher because daytime singers typically remain hidden from view, and at night all is shrouded in darkness. Persistent effort, coupled with help from this book and compact disc, will allow you to gradually unravel the chorus, and soon you will be able to identify the many "instruments" that contribute to the performance. Once deciphered, we are confident that the orchestra of insect sounds will delight your spirit as never before and shower you with auditory pleasures untold.

Classification of Singing Insects

Our native insect musicians, with the exception of the cicadas, are members of four families within the insect order Orthoptera.* The family Gryllidae includes the field crickets and ground crickets (both possessing the familiar cricket body plan), as well as the lesser-known tree crickets, bush crickets, and trigs. The family Gryllotalpidae is represented by the mole crickets, chunky creatures with forelegs adapted for burrowing. The family Tettigoniidae includes a wide variety of katydids, including the meadow katydids, true and false katydids, coneheads, and shieldbacks, which range in color from green to gray and have long filamentous antennae. Because of their long antennae and grasshopper-like body shapes, katydids are sometimes referred to as "long-horned grasshoppers." The family Acrididae includes the large number of grasshoppers, or locusts, with short antennae that are commonly found hopping about in grassy meadows in late summer. Because of their short antennae, they are sometimes referred to as "short-horned grasshoppers." In this book, we will use both "grasshopper" and "locust" to refer to members of the family Acrididae.

The cicadas are members of the family Cicadidae, which is in the order Homoptera (or Hemiptera, according to some taxonomists). Cicadas are closely related to leafhoppers, aphids, and scale insects and have little in common with members of the order Orthoptera. Unfortunately, many laypeople inappropriately refer to cicadas as locusts, especially in reference to periodical cicadas, which may suddenly appear in great numbers and remind people of the population explosions of certain locusts (grasshoppers) that are responsible for extensive crop damage in many parts of the world. To avoid confusion, the word "locust" should never be used as a synonym for "cicada."

Fall Field Cricket (singing male)

*There are differences of opinion concerning classification of members of the order Orthoptera. In fact, some taxonomists actually place the crickets and katydids in their own order, Grylloptera. In this book, we have adopted what we believe to be the most widespread and conservative classification scheme.

A Visual Guide to the Insect Musicians

Order Orthoptera — Crickets, Katydids, and Grasshoppers

Families Gryllidae and Gryllotalpidae — Crickets, Mole Crickets, and Trigs

Field Crickets

Bush Crickets

Ground Crickets

Tree Crickets

Mole Crickets

Trigs

Family Tettigoniidae — Katydids (Long-horned Grasshoppers)

Meadow Katydids

Conehead Katydids

True Katydids

Family Tettigoniidae *(continued)*

False Katydids   Shieldback Katydids

Family Acrididae — Grasshoppers (Locusts or Short-horned Grasshoppers)

Slant-faced Grasshoppers   Band-winged Grasshoppers

Order Homoptera — Cicadas, Leafhoppers, and Aphids

Family Cicadidae — Cicadas

Annual Cicadas   Periodical Cicadas

Biology of Insect Songs

Singing insects produce sounds in a variety of ways. Members of the order Orthoptera typically create sound by "stridulation," which is the rubbing of one body part against the other. Among crickets and katy-

file and scraper area of a Common True Katydid

dids, the base of the forewings is specially modified for sound production. A sharp edge, or "scraper," at the base of one front wing is rubbed across a bumpy ridge, or "file," located at the base of the opposite wing (see close-up photo on the facing page). Sounds produced in this fashion range from the melodic trills or chirps of crickets to the high-pitched raspy squawks, buzzes, and shuffles of katydids and grasshoppers.

During sound production, crickets and katydids elevate their wings and then move them back and forth rapidly. The wings vibrate to produce the song. Among field and ground crickets, the wings are held up at a low angle from the body and spread slightly dur-

Snowy Tree Cricket singing

ing song, while in the tree crickets they are held straight up at a right angle to the body. Among the katydids, singing postures can be subtle, with wings held up only slightly when the insect is singing.

Although many of our native grasshoppers (Acrididae) do not stridulate, a number produce sounds by rubbing their hind legs against

Fall Field Cricket singing

the edges of the forewings. Short peglike bumps on their hind femurs function something like a file. Singing males can be recognized by the rapid up-and-down movement of their hind legs, and sounds produced in this fashion are typically soft and rasping in quality. Band-winged Grasshoppers may also "crepitate" in flight by flashing their colored hindwings and snapping them together to produce crackling or buzzing sounds.

In contrast to the Orthopterans, male cicadas have a pair of special sound-producing organs, or "tymbals," located at the sides of the basal abdominal segment. The contraction of muscles causes ribs in the tymbals to bend suddenly and produce sound that resonates inside a large tracheal air sac in the abdomen. Cicadas produce very loud and penetrating sounds, far surpassing the songs of most Orthopterans in terms of sheer volume and the distance at which they can be heard.

close-up of file and scraper of a Common True Katydid

Sword-bearing Conehead singing

INSECT HEARING

The singing Orthopterans possess oval eardrums, or "tympana," which are characterized by a localized thinning of the cuticle at the site of the hearing organ. Crickets and katydids have tympana located on the front legs at the base of the tibia. Locusts have tympana covered by the wings and located on the sides of the first abdominal segment. Cicadas have exposed eardrums located on their abdomen next to their tymbals.

eardrums on a Northern Bush Katydid's forelegs

In general, the tympana of singing insects are relatively insensitive to changes in pitch but are very sensitive to changes in the intensity of the sounds being received. This corresponds to the basic structure of most insect songs, which rely more on variations in timing than on changes in pitch.

SONG STRUCTURE AND RECOGNITION

Most insect songs fall within the frequency range of 2,000–15,000 Hz and beyond (Hz = cycles per second). Crickets generally produce musical trills or chirps that fall on a definite pitch that is usually below 10,000 Hz. A trill is defined as a continuous train of notes or pulses given too fast to count and usually lasting several seconds or more. A chirp is a very short burst of notes (a very short trill lasting a fraction of a second), usually given in a series, with each chirp being followed by a brief period of silence.

Katydids and grasshoppers alike have high-pitched songs that contain a wide band of frequencies, with emphasis often falling above 10,000 Hz. Many are nearly or quite inaudible, especially if the listener has high-frequency hearing loss (see page 27). The songs are variously described as being noiselike and composed of atonal shuffles, rattles, scrapes, swishes, buzzes, or ticks, depending on the species. Some species, such as many of the meadow katydids, sing more or less continuously. Others, such as a number of the false katydids, sing intermittently, with long periods of silence between singing bouts.

Cicadas are known for their loud and penetrating songs. Most fall below 10,000 Hz and are variously described as rattling buzzes or harsh trills, and they often have a pulsating or grinding quality. In many species, song starts slowly, builds to a crescendo, and then finally drops off at the end.

Each species has its own distinct song, which is recognized by all individuals of the same species. Songs are told apart both by their dominant frequency and by the details of their timing patterns. It is important to note, however, that singing insects are cold-blooded and that the pulse rates of their songs vary with temperature.

Songs tend to speed up as the temperature rises and slow down as the temperature falls. Thus, the song of each species must be defined with respect to the ambient temperature.

Insects are not at all confused by this. Apparently, as the temperature of an insect changes, so does its "idea" of what determines its own species' song. In other words, its notion of the proper pulse rate of the song of its species rises proportionally with a rise in temperature and drops proportionally with a drop in temperature. Because of this effect, the songs of certain species can actually be used to approximate the temperature. A well-known example is the Snowy Tree Cricket (page 60). An early researcher determined that counting the number of chirps given in fifteen seconds and then adding 40 gives a close approximation to the actual temperature in degrees Fahrenheit. Likewise, similar formulas can be determined for a variety of species of singing insects.

Snowy Tree Cricket

FUNCTIONS OF SONGS

The great majority of insect songs that we hear in nature are the "calling songs" of males, produced primarily to attract mates. Calling songs may have other functions as well. In some species, the calling song may serve to attract males to a group chorus whose combined sounds attract females to the area (this occurs among many cicadas). Alternatively, the mating song may function to keep males optimally dispersed within singing colonies (this occurs among many meadow katydids, coneheads, and cicadas).

Males of certain species, especially field crickets, also have special "courtship songs," which are given in the presence of a female. These often sound similar to the calling song but with obvious changes in the timing. For instance, in the Spring and Fall Field Crickets, the calling song is a measured series of repeated chirps, while the courtship song is a sputtering ramble of rapidly delivered notes. Some species also give "aggressive sounds," made when two males encounter one another. Field crickets are a good example. Certain species may also respond with "disturbance calls" when handled. For instance, Common True Katydids may give loud raspy calls when touched, and many cicadas respond with rattling squawks. At least among cicadas, one individual giving a disturbance call may cause other nearby individuals to quit singing and fly away.

Female calling is rare among Orthopterans and cicadas, but there are cases in which females respond with special calls to the calling songs of the males. For instance, in the Greater Anglewing, females often follow the male's song with a sharp *tick*. Similarly, female cicadas of many species may respond to a nearby male with a sharp snap, produced by shuffling their wings.

COURTSHIP, MATING, AND LIFE CYCLE

Among most of our singing insects, the male attracts a female by singing his calling song (see "Functions of Songs," at left). When he becomes aware of her approach, he either stops singing altogether or switches to a special "courtship song" that further engages the female. In crickets and katydids, it is not uncommon for the male to vibrate his body at this point, a behavior known as "tremulation," which helps the female orient herself for mating. The male not only offers the female a sperm packet (spermatophore), but also may offer her a "nutritional gift" intended for consumption during mating.

In the photograph below of a pair of mating Broad-winged Tree Crickets, the female has climbed on top of the male (this is the case for most crickets) and is feeding on secretions from glands on his back as he prepares to transfer a spermatophore from the tip of his tail to her tail.

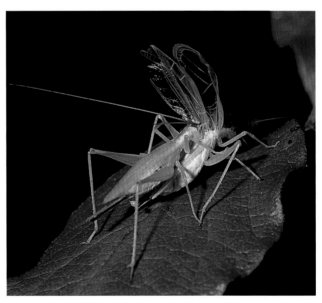

Broad-winged Tree Crickets mating

In katydids, the sequence is often different, but the outcome is the same. For example, the male may approach the female from behind and clasp her abdomen. In the photograph below of mating Fork-tailed Bush Katydids, the male on the left is transferring a spermatophore to the female on the right. The glob is composed of his sperm packet plus a much larger edible gelatinous mass that she will eat once the male has disengaged.

Fork-tailed Bush Katydids copulating

Cicadas follow a similar pattern, but they often fly about in search of females. In Linnaeus's 17-year Cicada, the courtship sequence is complex. In his search for a female within dense congregations of other calling males, the male flies from perch to perch, calling from each location for short periods. If a receptive female is nearby, she responds to his song by flicking her wings to make a high-pitched snap or *tick.* Upon hearing this sound, the male begins singing a special courtship song that elicits more ticks and guides him to the female. Finally, he mounts his mate and begins singing yet a third song type as the pair join to accomplish sperm transfer.

The photograph below shows a pair copulating. As with crickets and katydids, pairs separate after copulation, and males are able to mate with other females they encounter during the breeding period.

In all the singing insects, mated females immediately begin searching for good places to lay their eggs. In crickets and katydids, eggs are laid either in the soil or in plant tissues. Grasshoppers (locusts) usually lay their eggs in soil, while most cicadas lay their eggs in the woody stems of trees and shrubs.

In nearly all species of crickets, katydids, and grasshoppers, the eggs do not hatch until spring, when young nymphs emerge that

mating pair of
Linnaeus's 17-year Cicadas

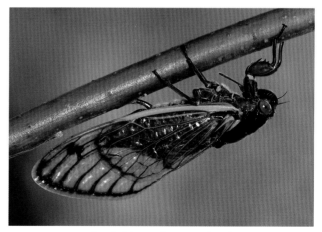

female Linnaeus's 17-year Cicada
inserting ovipositor in stem

nymphal female bush katydid having just shed its skin

feed, grow, and shed their skin as they pass through five or more instar stages before becoming sexually mature adults (which is why we don't hear many singing insects until the last half of the summer). Some species, such as the Spring Field Cricket, may overwinter as nymphs, and there are cases in which adults survive the winter, especially in the southern states. Cicada eggs typically hatch in late summer or early autumn. The nymphs fall to the ground and burrow into the earth, where they subsist on roots for several years as they pass through their instar stages. Just before becoming adults, they emerge from the ground, crawl up tree trunks, and then shed their last skin. Nymphal skins are easy to find in areas where cicadas are common.

DAILY PATTERNS OF SINGING

During warm days from midsummer into autumn, insects can be heard singing at all times during the day and night. However, many species show marked daily rhythms in song production.

In general, field and ground crickets can be heard singing almost anytime during the day and night. Tree crickets and most katydids sing primarily at night (especially during the first half of the night), although a number of species commonly sing during the day. In contrast, the grasshoppers (locusts) are exclusively day singers, and most actually prefer the hottest times of the day.

Cicadas are day singers, and many show a preference for a particular time of day. Some sing mostly in the morning and taper off by midday (Linnaeus's 17-year Cicada), while others do not sing until late in the afternoon or at dusk (such as the Northern Dusk-singing Cicada). All species of cicadas quit singing at dark, at which time the insect chorus becomes dominated by the songs of crickets and katydids.

Night-singing crickets and katydids do most of their calling in the first few hours after darkness, with little calling after midnight in many species. Late in the season, when nights become too cold for most insects to sing, many will adjust by singing late in the day or at dusk, before the temperature plummets.

Linne's Cicada emerging from skin

CHORUSING BEHAVIOR

A number of species tend to form singing aggregations, in which males group together within appropriate habitats. Various cicadas exhibit this behavior. For example, it has been shown that male Linnaeus's 17-year Cicadas are attracted to one another's calls and hence form dense choruses. Certain meadow katydids also tend to occur in colonies, but males are usually well spaced within a colony. Such aggregations could be the result of habitat preferences but often consist of more individuals than one might expect based on habitat quality alone.

Within colonies, calling often has contagious elements. For instance, the first male to begin singing in a group often elicits singing in other males. This is particularly noticeable among certain bush katydids. In the Broad-winged Bush Katydid, individual males give their song sequence intermittently, with several minutes of silence in between. In this species there is a marked tendency for males in a colony to sound off in a loosely coordinated sequence. When one male begins singing, another follows, then another, and so forth.

Singing insects may also synchronize their songs. For instance, in the Common Meadow Katydid, the song is

Common True Katydid

composed of a series of *ticks* followed by a buzz. Individuals in dense colonies often synchronize their songs so that they are all ticking together and then buzzing together. Likewise, neighboring male Snowy Tree Crickets often sing in unison, and it is not uncommon to find a number of males chirping together in almost perfect synchrony. Synchrony also occurs in the Nebraska Conehead. In the Columbian Trig, males in colonies call together but synchronize imperfectly, to create a unique throbbing sound.

A complicated example of alternation and synchrony occurs in the Common True Katydid. Neighboring males tend to alternate their calls. But when a large number of katydids are close enough to react to one another, the result is a combination of alternation and synchrony in which each male is alternating with the neighbor he hears most clearly, but is at the same time synchronized with other males who are alternating with the same neighbor. The result is a huge pulsing soundscape that is rather amazing to behold.

Columbian Trig (immature female)

Appreciation and Aesthetics

For many centuries, a deep appreciation of insect song has been evident in Asian cultures, especially in China and Japan, where insect musicians have long been celebrated by the poets. In ancient times, city dwellers would take autumn vacations to remote areas of the countryside in order to appreciate particular insect songs or choruses known for their inherent beauty.* By the sixteenth century, *mushiya* (insect sellers) were commonly found in the outdoor markets of cities, and it became fashionable to keep singing crickets and katydids as pets, for the sheer aesthetic pleasure of hearing their songs through the winter months, long after they had become silent out-of-doors. The finest singers were given endearing names that described their songs or habitats, such as *jin zhong* (golden bell), *jiao ge-ge* (singing brother), *kusa-hiban* (grass lark), *yabu-suzu* (little bell of the bamboo grove), and *aki-kaze* (autumn wind). These names demonstrate an aesthetic sensibility that is well refined.

In comparison to the Asian fascination with insect songs, which remained prevalent through the 1800s, our culture shows far less refinement. Certainly, we perceive and enjoy the pulsing choruses of late summer and autumn, but aside from a few outstanding species (such as the Common True Katydid and the Spring and Fall Field Crickets), most of us seem perpetually confused about which insect is making which sound, and we have no established aesthetic that helps us enjoy the beauty and communicate our appreciation to others.

We are optimistic that our book will help change this situation. With the help of this practical guide to our most common species, it is now possible for anyone who is interested to decipher the chorus and gain an appreciation of the diversity of songs and the extraordinary beauty of the singers themselves. We have further expanded upon this theme by founding a new organization, the Society for the Appreciation of Insect Songs, whose Internet home is www.insectsongs.org. Visit our Web site and sign on.

As part of the unfolding of this new aesthetic, we encourage readers to learn how to find the singers in order to see what they look like. We also approve of capturing a small assortment of "desired" species and keeping them in captivity, in order to enjoy their songs long after frosts have killed adults in the wild. For more information on this topic, refer to "Finding, Collecting, and Keeping Insects" on page 214.

These are exciting times. As people far and wide come to a full appreciation of our insect musicians, interest will explode and a new industry will be spawned. Before long, hundreds of thousands of nature enthusiasts will be tuned in, and nearly all will be planning outings and vacations to experience the glory of the insect soundscape. We are confident that this will come to pass, and we invite you to join in the fun!

---

*A terrific source of information about the appreciation of insect songs in Japan and China, and the source of historical information presented in this section, is *Insect Musicians and Cricket Champions: A Cultural History of Singing Insects in China and Japan,* by Lisa Gail Ryan.

Texas Bush Katydid

Human Perception of Insect Songs

The full appreciation of insect songs lies in the province of the young, who still have youthful hearing with full high-frequency response. But even youthful ears can be strained, as certain insects sing at the very upper register of human hearing and often beyond. Sadly, as we age, most of us lose our high-frequency sensitivity, and by middle-age or beyond, many of us can no longer hear the highest singers. What was once a meadow or hedgerow resounding with the high-pitched trills, chirps, shuffles, crackles, and ticks of insect singers may be transformed into a quiet pastoral scene, punctuated only by the soft rustle of grass swaying in a gentle breeze.

The numbers don't lie. Youthful human hearing extends from around 30 Hz to as high as 20,000 Hz. Frequency range is best explained in terms of octaves, which involves a doubling of the frequency. Thus, human hearing covers a little more than nine octaves approximated by the following ranges in Hz: 30–60, 60–125, 125–250, 250–500, 500–1,000, 1,000–2,000, 2,000–4,000, 4,000–8,000, and 8,000–16,000 and higher. Most insect sounds occur in the upper two octaves of human hearing, primarily from around 4,000 Hz to 20,000 Hz. Thus, a young person with "normal" hearing will be aware of most of the insect singers in his surroundings.

Unfortunately, high-pitched sensitivity gradually declines as we age, a phenomenon known as "presbycusis." In fact, by age fifty many of us are no longer very sensitive to sounds of 10,000 Hz and above. By age sixty, the situation worsens, and moderate to severe hearing loss above 5,000 Hz is not uncommon. The sad truth is that someone suffering from such hearing loss may hear only a small fraction of the insect sounds in his surroundings,

even though perception of human speech remains relatively unaffected. Hearing loss due to aging is not fully understood, but it may involve the continued unnatural exposure to the loud sounds of our modern society. Aspiring young naturalists and adults alike should do everything possible to protect their hearing. This means wearing earplugs in noisy situations, avoiding prolonged exposure to high noise levels, and shunning any activity that hurts the ears. Under no circumstances should one do anything that results in ringing of the ears, as this is a sure sign of nerves being damaged.

Until recently, there was little someone could do to bring back the songs of the insects. Conventional amplifying-type hearing aids may help with the lowest singers, but such hearing aids are primarily designed to enhance speech perception at frequencies below 5,000 Hz — most insects sing higher than that. Various bat detectors are now available, and they should also work well with insects, especially those singing at the highest frequencies. Another solution is the SongFinder (www.hearbirds-again.com), a digital device designed for nature lovers that lowers high-frequency bird and insect sounds into a range where one's hearing is still normal.

*Short-winged Meadow Katydid
(has a song frequency of 10–20 kHz)*

Marsh Meadow Grasshopper (peak song frequency is about 16 kHz)

About Sonagrams

Each species profile in this book includes one or two sound pictures, or "sonagrams," depicting the song of the male. Technically referred to as a "sound spectrogram," the sonagram was developed for the scientific study of sounds. The result is an intuitive graphical representation that roughly resembles the way we depict music on a musical staff. Refer to the examples below. The horizontal axis of a sonagram represents time in seconds, and the vertical axis represents the pitch or frequency of the sound in kilohertz (kHz). One kHz is equivalent to 1,000 hertz (Hz) or 1,000 cycles/second (middle C on a piano is 440 Hz and the highest key on a piano is 4,000 Hz, or 4 kHz). In most cases, we simplify the frequency axis somewhat by including only one number (rarely two or three) that conveys the dominant frequency or frequency range of an insect's song. In this book, insect songs range from as low as 2,000 Hz for the Northern Mole Cricket to 15–20 kHz for some meadow katydids and shieldbacks that sing at the upper limit of youthful human hearing.

Unlike the musical staff, which conveys notes of a particular frequency, the sonagram depicts everything from pure tones to nonmusical harsh sounds that cover a broad frequency range. A pure tone would be represented as a horizontal band or line with a narrow width, and a click would be a simple vertical line of limited width. None of our native insects produce songs that are extended pure tones, but many crickets produce musical notes of limited bandwidth delivered in a rapid series or trill, such as the song of the Black-horned Tree Cricket (pictured opposite). In contrast to musical sounds, broadband noises have a wide frequency span. Most of our katydids produce nonmusical sounds of this type, such as the song of the Common True Katydid pictured below, which extends from around 4 kHz upward to 15 kHz and above. Sound elements that are rapidly repeated might sound like a musical trill, a dry trill, a swishy rattle, a shuffling purr, or a buzz, depending on their frequency structure and repetition rate. While the reader is not expected to infer the quality of an insect's sound merely by looking at a sonagram, sound pictures do provide useful impressions and can be enjoyed in their own right, as graphic and artistic expressions of the sounds that insects make.

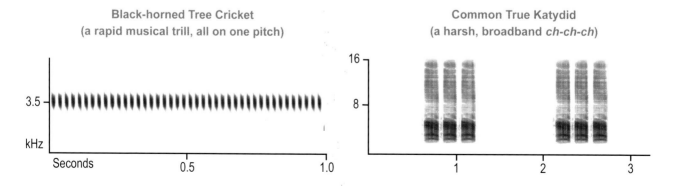

Black-horned Tree Cricket
(a rapid musical trill, all on one pitch)

3.5 —

kHz

Seconds   0.5   1.0

Common True Katydid
(a harsh, broadband *ch-ch-ch*)

16

8

1   2   3

Black-horned Tree Cricket (singing)

The Compact Disc

The audio compact disc that accompanies this book has been carefully crafted to provide the reader with excellent examples of the insect sounds that are described here. Each recording includes a brief narrated introduction by Wil Hershberger. The tracks on the disc correspond to the seventy-five species profile numbers, as presented in the list on the following two pages and in the upper left corner of each species page spread.

Broad-winged Bush Katydid

THE RANGE MAPS

The range maps show likely general distributions of each species, as determined by scientific records of collected specimens. Refer to Tom Walker's Web site for detailed versions of these maps: www.buzz.ifas.ufl.edu.

LENGTHS

Lengths for each species, given in inches, indicate the distance from the head to the tip of the abdomen in short-winged species (not counting reproductive parts such as female ovipositors), or from the head to the tip of the wing in long-winged insects. In many species, females are longer on average than males. Lengths of insects included in this book range from about ¼ inch for the Say's Trig and other trigs to almost 3 inches for female Robust Coneheads.

TEMPERATURE AND SONG RATES

When pulse rates, chirp rates, song lengths, or other aspects of tempo are presented in this guide, the values represent the rate or timing that occurs at around room temperature, or 76°F (23°C).

FREQUENCIES OF SONGS

When describing each species' song, we generally give the primary frequency of the song, or else its frequency range, both derived from the study of sonagrams. We were able to measure up to 20 kHz, the upper limit of human hearing, and also the upper limit of our digital recordings and our sonagrams. In cases in which we describe a song as having a range that goes up to 20 kHz, be aware that there also may be song components extending well above 20 kHz, outside the range of human hearing.

Species List

The numbers refer to the seventy-five species profiles and are equivalent to track numbers on the compact disc.

CRICKETS

Field Crickets and Bush Crickets

1. Spring Field Cricket and Fall Field Cricket — *Gryllus veletis* and *Gryllus pennsylvanicus*
2. Southeastern Field Cricket — *Gryllus rubens*
3. Eastern Striped Cricket — *Miogryllus saussurei*
4. Jumping Bush Cricket — *Orocharis saltator*

Ground Crickets

5. Carolina Ground Cricket — *Eunemobius carolinus*
6. Allard's Ground Cricket — *Allonemobius allardi*
7. Tinkling Ground Cricket — *Allonemobius tinnulus*
8. Striped Ground Cricket — *Allonemobius fasciatus*
9. Confused Ground Cricket — *Eunemobius confusus*
10. Sphagnum Ground Cricket — *Neonemobius palustris*

Tree Crickets

11. Snowy Tree Cricket — *Oecanthus fultoni*
12. Broad-winged Tree Cricket — *Oecanthus latipennis*
13. Fast-calling Tree Cricket — *Oecanthus celerinictus*
14. Black-horned Tree Cricket — *Oecanthus nigricornis*
15. Pine Tree Cricket — *Oecanthus pini*
16. Four-spotted Tree Cricket — *Oecanthus quadripunctatus*
17. Davis's Tree Cricket — *Oecanthus exclamationis*
18. Narrow-winged Tree Cricket — *Oecanthus niveus*
19. Two-spotted Tree Cricket — *Neoxabea bipunctata*

Mole Crickets

20. Northern Mole Cricket — *Neocurtilla hexadactyla*
21. Southern Mole Cricket — *Scapteriscus borellii*

Trigs

22. Say's Trig — *Anaxipha exigua*
23. Columbian Trig — *Cyrtoxipha columbiana*
24. Handsome Trig — *Phyllopalpus pulchellus*

KATYDIDS (Long-horned Grasshoppers)

Meadow Katydids

25. Short-winged Meadow Katydid — *Conocephalus brevipennis*
26. Slender Meadow Katydid — *Conocephalus fasciatus*
27. Woodland Meadow Katydid — *Conocephalus nemoralis*
28. Saltmarsh Meadow Katydid — *Conocephalus spartinae*
29. Straight-lanced Meadow Katydid — *Conocephalus strictus*
30. Handsome Meadow Katydid — *Orchelimum pulchellum*
31. Black-legged Meadow Katydid — *Orchelimum nigripes*
32. Agile Meadow Katydid — *Orchelimum agile*
33. Red-headed Meadow Katydid — *Orchelimum erythrocephalum*
34. Common Meadow Katydid — *Orchelimum vulgare*
35. Gladiator Meadow Katydid — *Orchelimum gladiator*
36. Lesser Pine Katydid — *Orchelimum minor*
37. Long-spurred Meadow Katydid — *Orchelimum silvaticum*

Conehead Katydids

38. Sword-bearing Conehead — *Neoconocephalus ensiger*
39. Slightly Musical Conehead — *Neoconocephalus exiliscanorus*
40. Nebraska Conehead — *Neoconocephalus nebrascensis*
41. Round-tipped Conehead — *Neoconocephalus retusus*
42. Robust Conehead — *Neoconocephalus robustus*

True Katydids

43. Common True Katydid — *Pterophylla camellifolia*

Least Shieldback

Texas Bush Katydid

Field Crickets and Bush Crickets
Gryllus, Miogryllus, Orocharis, and *Hapithus*

You've seen them, the robust black crickets with round heads that invade your household, especially in the autumn. These are the field crickets, endearing creatures looking for a cozy home. There are about twenty native species in North America (north of Mexico), represented by five genera, with thirteen species in our region. Three wide-ranging field crickets are profiled in this book, two being members of the genus *Gryllus,* the most-studied group of all our singing insects. While the majority of our native field crickets are shiny black in color, there are exceptions, such as the gorgeous Eastern Striped Cricket *(Miogryllus saussurei),* which sports a coat of dark brown and cream. In addition to our native field crickets, there are several introduced species, including the brown-colored House Cricket *(Acheta domesticus),* an Asian cricket that is sold for fish bait and as pet food (it is not covered in this guide).

Field crickets are found in nearly every habitat that has sufficient moisture. From rock crevices in city sidewalks to grassy patches among sand dunes at the beach, their songs fill the summer air from June until frost. Most species either chirp or trill, and songs usually have a me-lodic quality. Singing males can be difficult to find, as they hide under rocks, leaves, and other debris, and go silent whenever they are disturbed. Interestingly, most male field crickets, and males of other cricket groups as well, are "right-handed singers," meaning that their right forewing sits on top of their left forewing (in contrast, most male katydids are "left-handed singers").

In comparison to the field and striped crickets, our native bush crickets are members of a different group and have a different appearance, with colors ranging from reddish brown to gray (see photos below). There are eleven species in North America (north of Mexico), representing four genera. But most are restricted in range to the southeastern coastal plain or else to peninsular Florida. Two species range more widely, including the Jumping Bush Cricket *(Orocharis saltator)* and the Restless Bush Cricket *(Hapithus agitator).* The former is very vocal with a chirping song, and we cover it in this guide. In contrast, the Restless Bush Cricket does not sing over most of its range (although males in peninsular Florida and eastern Texas do sing), so we decided not to include it in our profiles.

Jumping Bush Cricket   *Restless Bush Cricket*

1. Spring and Fall Field Crickets *Gryllus veletis* and *G. pennsylvanicus (2/3")*

The Spring and Fall Field Crickets look and sound the same—they are large, black, and round-headed, and their song is the quintessential cricket chirp. The two species were once thought to be the same, but scientific studies revealed that there are indeed two different species that are morphologically almost identical but developmentally different—Fall Field Crickets overwinter as eggs and Spring Field Crickets as nymphs. In areas where both species are found, they are best identified by when they are seen or heard. Because they overwinter as nymphs, Spring Field Crickets develop quickly when warm weather arrives, and adults typically appear and begin singing and mating in late spring, continuing until late June or early July, when they die off. In contrast, Fall Field Crickets hatch in the spring, and adults don't appear and begin singing until mid- or late July, after which they continue singing into the autumn, when they are finally killed by frosts. In most areas of overlap, there is a period of silence in midsummer when neither species is heard.

Both species are found in a wide variety of habitats and are common around buildings, where they hide in cracks and crevices, under rocks, or in shal-

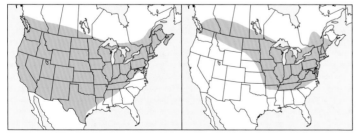

Fall Field Cricket   Spring Field Cricket

singing male

low burrows. As winter approaches, Fall Field Crickets are attracted to heat and often find their way into houses or other buildings.

Song: The song of both species is a series of clear, loud chirps given at a rate of about one per second (or faster). Each chirp is actually a brief trill consisting of 3–5 pulses, given too fast for the human ear to detect. The frequency of the song is approximately 4–5 kHz, depending on the ambient temperature. Field crickets chirp both day and night from their hideouts but are typically quiet at dawn.

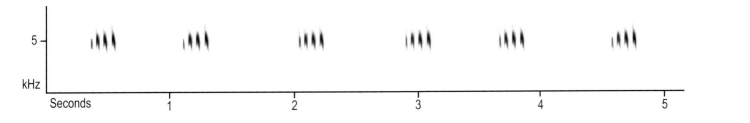

female with oviposotor

Resembling a small Spring or Fall Field Cricket, the Southeastern Field Cricket is one of only two North American field cricket species that produce a continuous trill (the other is *Gryllus texensis,* a look-alike western species). These crickets can have either long wings or short wings. Not well studied, this species was recently found in the eastern panhandle of West Virginia, a range extension of several hundred miles.

The Southeastern Field Cricket is very common in the southern portion of its range and is the most numerous field cricket in Florida. It favors disturbed grassy areas. The underwings are longer than the body, giving these crickets an odd appearance. One might even mistake a male, such as the one pictured above, for a female because the protruding underwings resemble a female's ovipositor.

Song: A continuous musical trill, sometimes given smoothly, but often interrupted by short pauses that give it a stuttering quality. The dominant frequency of the song is approximately 5 kHz.

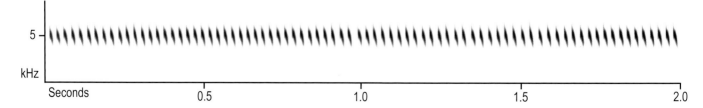

The Eastern Striped Cricket is small but very attractive, with a large head and striking patterns of blackish brown and cream colors that are best appreciated by viewing with a hand lens or other magnifier. It frequents grassy and weedy areas throughout its range. Singing males usually hide deep in a tangle of plant material at the soil surface, making these little crickets hard to find and capture. This species is highly variable and poorly studied and does not do well in captivity.

Song: Consists of brief buzzes at about 7 kHz, usually rising slightly in pitch and loudness from beginning to end, that are repeated every few seconds or so. The song is easily heard at close range but does not travel far. It also has a ventriloquial quality that makes locating the singer a challenge.

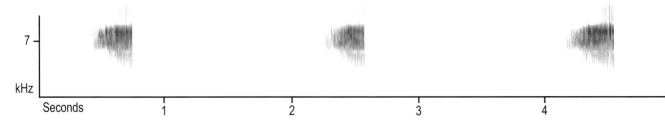

4. Jumping Bush Cricket *Orocharis saltator* (5/8″–3/4″)

O ften heard but seldom seen, the light brown Jumping Bush Cricket is a common inhabitant of rural and urban backyards. Named because it will jump when disturbed, the arboreal bush cricket has a unique flattened or compressed appearance. Males sing from vine-covered tree trunks or dense herbaceous growth, as well as from the crowns of trees. A careful search of tree trunks at night may reveal one singing from a partially concealed perch.

Song: A clear, brief trill or chirp, repeated at the rate of one or two per second. Neighboring males often sing at slightly different pitches, perhaps making them easier for females to locate. In late August they can be heard singing as soon as the sun goes down. Later in the season, after the first frosts, males sing from less concealed perches and may even be found on the sides of buildings near plantings. The frequency of songs is about 5 kHz.

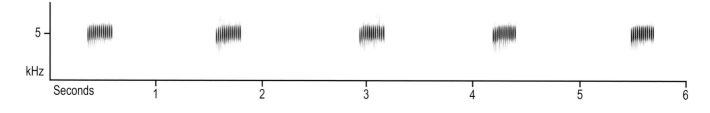

Ground Crickets
Eunemobius, Allonemobius, and *Neonemobius*

Have you ever walked across a grassy meadow or lawn and noticed large numbers of small black crickets scurrying to get out of your way? Did you think these must be "baby" crickets, because they appeared to be miniature versions of the larger field crickets that you've found in your home? It may come as a surprise that these are actually adult or near-adult crickets belonging to the ground cricket group, a diverse assemblage of twenty-five North American species (north of Mexico), representing five different genera (twenty-three species are found in our region). This guide presents six species from three genera, seemingly a small number, but these are the species most likely to be seen and heard in the wild.

Collectively, the ground crickets are characterized by their small size and black or dark brown bodies and by their loud, musical trills and chirps. In appropriate habitat, they may be extremely abundant (for instance, if you own a swimming pool placed level with your lawn, you probably see a lot of them, especially after you mow, because they will hop across concrete walkways and fall into your pool and drown). Since ground crickets all look basically the same, identifying different species by sight is next to impossible. But many have preferred habitats, and nearly all can be distinguished by their songs.

A common song-theme for ground crickets is a continuous trill, but the trills of different species are delivered at different rates, and they also vary considerably in quality, ranging from melodious or tinkling to rather atonal or buzzy. Still other species produce a distinctive series of chirps or short trills. Although male ground crickets sing loudly, they remain well hidden and are a challenge to find and collect. When disturbed, they either retreat into nooks and crannies or else try to run or hop away. You can collect them by chasing or coaxing them into a vial or small jar, driving them onto a net laid flat on the ground, or sweeping the grass with an insect net.

Carolina Ground Cricket

5. Carolina Ground Cricket *Eunemobius carolinus* (1/3″)

Aconstant companion to grigologists throughout our region (a grigologist is someone who studies crickets, katydids, and cicadas), the widespread Carolina Ground Cricket can be found in almost every terrestrial habitat. They are very cold-tolerant and will be the last ground cricket singing as winter wraps its icy grip on the land. The song is surprisingly loud for such a small cricket, and getting a good location on a singer can be difficult. They can often be captured by turning over rocks or other debris in the vicinity of a singing male.

Song: A rapid, buzzy trill with a stumbling or sputtering quality, as if the singer is never quite able to get on track. This wavering quality is due to slight variations in loudness as well as pulse rate. Pulses are delivered at 50–60 per second (four or five times faster than the Allard's Ground Cricket) with a frequency of around 6 kHz.

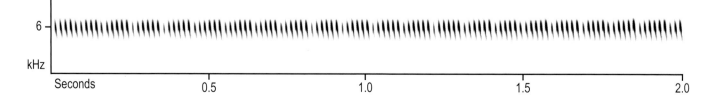

6. Allard's Ground Cricket *Allonemobius allardi* (3/8″)

The cheery trilling of the Allard's Ground Cricket is a sure sign of summer. Named after naturalist Harry A. Allard (1880–1963), who studied stridulation in insects, these small black crickets can be seen scurrying away from your feet as you walk in dry, open grassy areas. Close inspection reveals that individuals are covered with long hairs used to constantly monitor their surroundings. Favored habitats include lawns, parks, pastures, and roadsides. When cold weather arrives, these little crickets often find their way into houses. It is a pleasant surprise to suddenly hear a male Allard's singing his lovely song from inside your home.

Song: A continuous, even trill composed of pulses given at a rate of 10–16 per second (too fast to count), with a dominant frequency of about 6 kHz. Pleasing to the ear. In contrast, males give sputtery trills when they interact.

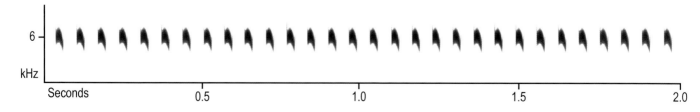

7. Tinkling Ground Cricket *Allonemobius tinnulus* (3/8″)

Walking deep within the hardwoods of the eastern and midwestern states, one often hears lovely tinkling notes coming from the leaf litter. This is the haunt of the Tinkling Ground Cricket. He is the deep woods counterpart to the Allard's Ground Cricket, and he can usually be recognized by the slow pace of his song.

Song: A series of bright tinkling notes, given at an even tempo, generally slow enough to count. Pulse rates vary from 5 to 8 per second, depending on temperature. The dominant frequency is about 7 kHz. Tinkling and Allard's sound similar but can be differentiated by habitat and pulse rate. However, a warm Tinkling may sing nearly as fast as a cold Allard's, so exercise caution, especially in oak woods where there are open, grassy areas. Of course, it is great fun to be in a location where you can hear both species at the same time and note the distinctive difference in their songs.

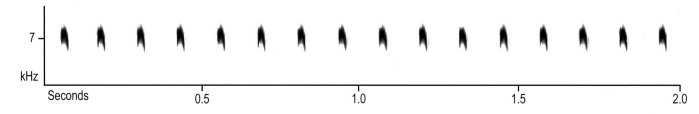

8. Striped Ground Cricket *Allonemobius fasciatus* (1/4″–3/8″)

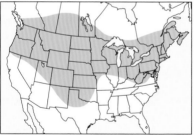

Striped Ground Crickets can be extremely numerous in damp grassy areas and the weedy edges of streams and ponds, where their sweet pulsing songs provide a perfect adagio for a peaceful summer's day. If you approach their haunt, frightened crickets scurry away from your feet and take refuge in the litter layer at the surface of the soil, making them very difficult to capture. One productive method is to herd them onto a light-colored sheet, where they can be collected with ease.

Song: A regular series of high-pitched, metallic chirps (brief buzzes) given at a brisk rate of about two per second. Each buzz is made up of 10–15 pulses with a frequency of about 7 kHz. Distinctive and easy to learn.

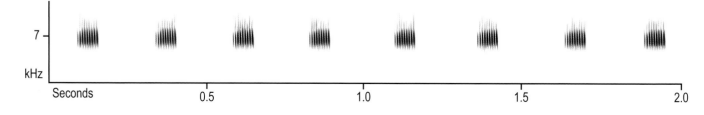

9. Confused Ground Cricket *Eunemobius confusus* (1/4″)

Certainly one of the most handsome of its group, the Confused Ground Cricket got its name from an early entomologist, Willis Blatchley (1859–1940), who initially "confused" it with the commonplace Carolina Ground Cricket. It is found in damp leaf litter under hardwoods. The best method for capturing these tiny and fast crickets is to locate a singing male, scoop up a large armful of leaf litter, and toss it onto a light-colored sheet spread out nearby. Sift through this tangle, and the singer will no doubt be revealed, usually hiding under the last piece of material to be removed.

Song: Produces a regular series of two-part trills lasting about a half second, occasionally interrupted by brief trills or chirps. The frequency is about 6 kHz. Males often position themselves under leaves in order to amplify and direct their songs, which are very loud for such a small cricket.

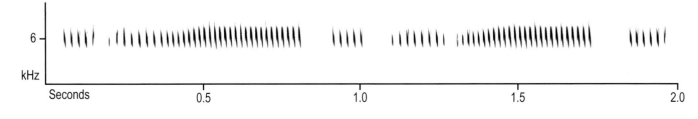

10. Sphagnum Ground Cricket   *Neonemobius palustris* (1/4″)

Not surprisingly, the Sphagnum Ground Cricket inhabits sphagnum bog lands, where it is often extremely common. The weak and high-pitched song is easily overlooked, but careful listening may reveal the constant din of multitudes of trilling crickets, especially on hot summer days in northern bogs. These tiny dark-brown crickets can be difficult to locate by their sounds. However, flooding a small area by pressing a hand into the sphagnum may reveal the little singers as they try to swim away.

Song: The song is a series of very high trills at about 9 kHz, with each trill lasting eight to thirteen seconds. The pulse rate of a trill is about 50 notes per second. Each trill starts softly and then gradually builds in volume, leveling off to full intensity about halfway through. Trills are separated by several seconds of silence.

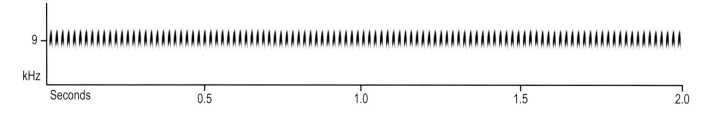

Tree Crickets
Oecanthus and *Neoxabea*

Most people think that all crickets look the same: compact, dark-colored, short-winged insects with body plans like those of the field crickets and ground crickets. So it may come as a surprise to learn that there is a group of crickets with an entirely different appearance—delicate creatures with translucent green or red-green bodies and long lacy wings that they hold straight up when they sing. These are the lovely tree crickets, whose pure-toned trills enliven the nighttime soundscape in a variety of habitats, from weedy fields and shrubby clearings to deciduous forests and pine woods. There are eighteen species of tree crickets in North America (north of Mexico), represented by two genera, and twelve of these are found in our region. We include profiles for nine of the most common and widespread species.

Among tree crickets, the dominant song pattern is a loud, continuous, musical trill. Species giving such trills are difficult to identify by song alone because the differences in pulse rate or frequency can be subtle (although with practice, these differences can be learned). But there are species that can easily be identified by song. For instance, the Snowy Tree Cricket gives a steady stream of distinctive melodious chirps, and the Narrow-winged and Two-Spotted Tree Crickets produce telltale broken trills. Interestingly, males of a number of species often sing from the underside of a curled leaf (see page 29), from the edge of a leaf (see opposite), or from a hole in a leaf (see below), in order to reduce acoustic interference and thereby increase the intensity of their songs.

Habitat can be a clue for identification—for instance, the Pine Tree Cricket sings almost exclusively from pine trees and the Broad-winged Tree Cricket sings from low vegetation such as goldenrods and bramble. Some tree crickets are also unique in appearance, but there are a number of look-alikes that can usually be separated by the pattern of black marks found on the basal segments of their antennae (see diagram on opposite page).

As briefly described on page 20, the mating behavior of tree crickets is fascinating. A male fiddles his tune to attract a female. Once she arrives, he raises his forewings to allow her to climb onto his back. At the base of his wings, there is a small pit or gland that exudes a sweet liquid, which the female begins devouring. While she is occupied, the male transfers a sperm packet to the female and his sperm slowly begins to make its way into her. The longer she feeds from his gland, the higher the probability that the male's sperm will fertilize her eggs.

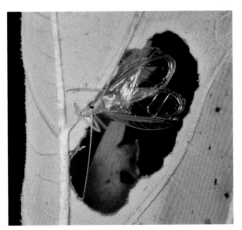

Four-spotted Tree Cricket
(singing from a hole in a leaf)

Broad-winged Tree Cricket
(singing from the edge of a leaf)

Snowy Tree Cricket
(close-up of the head showing antenna markings)

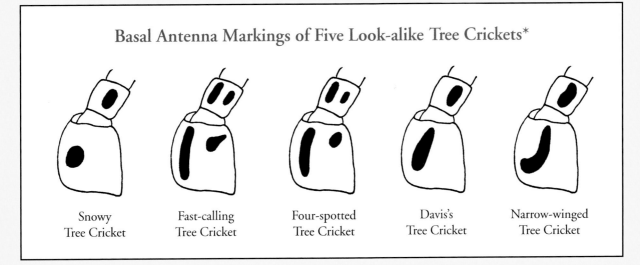

Basal Antenna Markings of Five Look-alike Tree Crickets*

Snowy
Tree Cricket

Fast-calling
Tree Cricket

Four-spotted
Tree Cricket

Davis's
Tree Cricket

Narrow-winged
Tree Cricket

*Redrawn from diagrams found in a variety of early scientific papers.

11. Snowy Tree Cricket *Oecanthus fultoni* (1/2"–3/4")

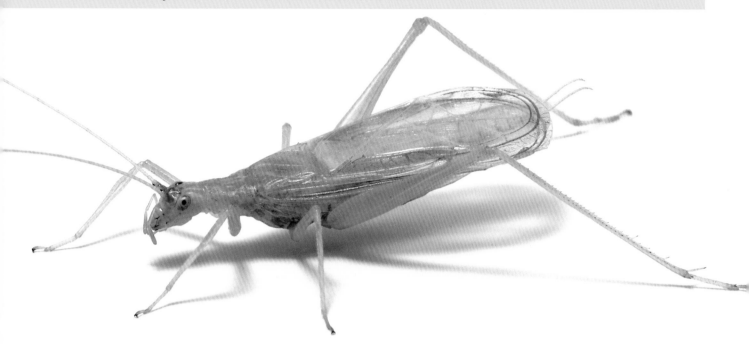

Perhaps the most familiar of our tree crickets, the Snowy Tree Cricket is the one whose chirp rate can easily be used to estimate the temperature. One popular formula is to count the number of songs given in thirteen seconds and then add that number to 40 to yield the temperature in degrees Fahrenheit. It is referred to as "snowy" because individuals are often so pale that they appear white. Snowy Tree Crickets sing from brushy understory plants at the margins of woods or within open woods. During cold spells, they can be found close to the ground on the trunks of small trees—here they probably find a warmer microenvironment.

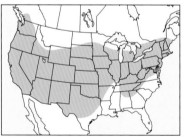

Song: Song is a very pleasant series of evenly spaced chirps, each chirp consisting of 8 (occasionally 5) pulses at a frequency of 3 kHz. Males prefer to sing from the underside of branches or broad leaves.

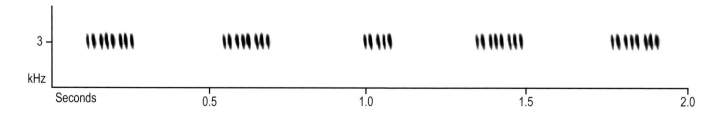

12. Broad-winged Tree Cricket *Oecanthus latipennis (2/3"–7/8")*

Named for its elegant, wide wings, the Broad-winged Tree Cricket sounds off in fields of coarse weeds from August through first frost. Favorite plants include goldenrod and bramble. A pleasing visual mix of cream-colored body and legs, light green wings, and reddish accents on the head and the base of the antennae combine to make this tree cricket stand out. Males sing from perches where they are able to use the surrounding vegetation to augment and direct their songs. They are often found low in the vegetation in the crotch of overlapping leaves, or else singing from a hole they have chewed in a leaf.

Song: Perhaps the loudest of the tree crickets. Males can be heard from two hundred feet away or more. Songs are pure-toned continuous trills that are rarely interrupted, with a main frequency of about 3 kHz and a pulse rate of about 25 per second. Males sing mostly at night, but after a light frost later in the season, they will sing early in the evening before the sunset.

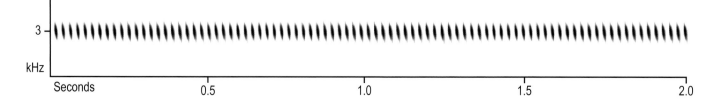

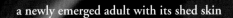

a newly emerged adult with its shed skin

Beautiful, elegant, and delicate are words that aptly describe the Fast-calling Tree Cricket. An inhabitant of weedy fields and roadsides, this species prefers broad-leafed plants, where individuals can sometimes be found during the day, perched in the open near the top of a plant. Finding a calling male at night is much more difficult because they perch lower and are very sensitive to disturbance. Color varies from pale reddish yellow to light green.

Song: As the common name implies, the song is a very rapid trill, with 65–70 pulses per second, generally delivered without pause. The frequency is about 4 kHz. This is one of the few tree crickets that regularly sing during the day. The song is loud and difficult to localize.

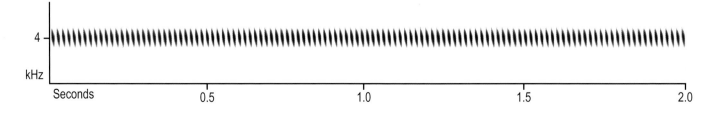

14. Black-horned Tree Cricket *Oecanthus nigricornis* (1/2″–2/3″)

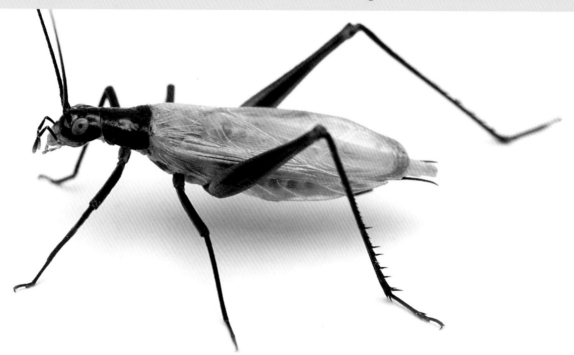

Unique in appearance among tree crickets, the Black-horned Tree Cricket is easily identified by the black markings on large portions of its body and legs. This species inhabits brushy fields and roadsides as well as bramble thickets. The males are fond of making a hole in a leaf by eating some of it and then using the hole as a singing perch. They may also sing from the underside of leaves (see page 29).

Song: A loud, continuous trill, consisting of about 45 pulses per second, with a frequency of about 3.5 kHz. Finding a singing male in a bush is truly an exercise in patience. He falls silent when disturbed and is nearly impossible to locate until he resumes singing several minutes later.

singing male

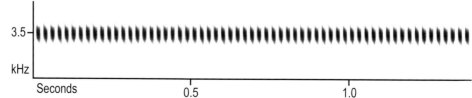

3.5 —

kHz

Seconds   0.5   1.0

female with ovipositor

Sporting a brownish red body and spruce-green wings, the Pine Tree Cricket is perhaps the most beautiful of all our tree crickets. This species is found almost exclusively in conifer trees, where its coloration helps it blend in, making it exceedingly difficult to observe or capture. After strong storms, however, these crickets may sometimes be found on vegetation in the shrub layer beneath preferred pines, cedars, and other evergreens. Males typically sing from a tangle of needles. As with other tree crickets, females seek out displaying males and can often be observed crawling on nearby limbs, moving in the direction of the singer.

Song: A continuous musical trill with about 45 pulses per second at a frequency of 3.5 kHz. Plaintive and relaxing. One of the most pleasing songs of all the tree crickets.

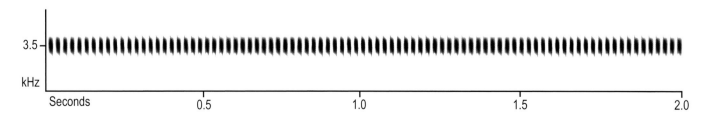

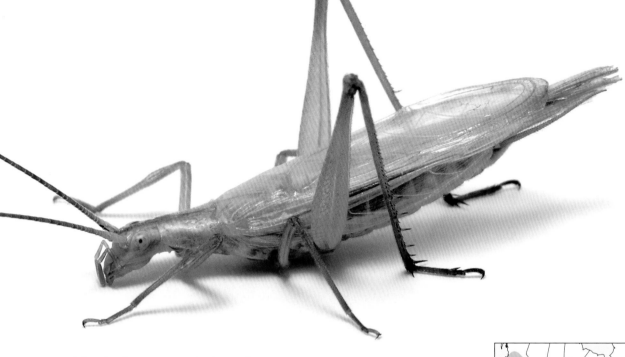

Named for the four spots at the base of its antennae (see page 59), the Four-Spotted Tree Cricket is greenish brown in color and is an inhabitant of fields of coarse weeds. This widespread species can be very common and is markedly tolerant of minor disturbances and lights. It is rewarding to find these lovely tree crickets in a meadow at night and watch a male singing at close range. You may also notice an approaching female (see photo in upper left of opposite page) and be lucky enough to observe the entire mating sequence.

Song: A continuous trill of about 40 pulses per second at a frequency of 4 kHz. Given both day and night.

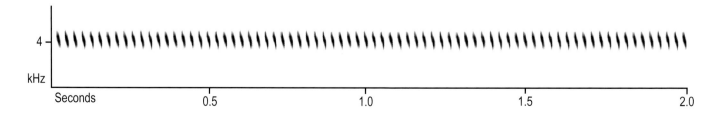

female approaching a singing male

17. Davis's Tree Cricket *Oecanthus exclamationis* (1/2″–3/4″)

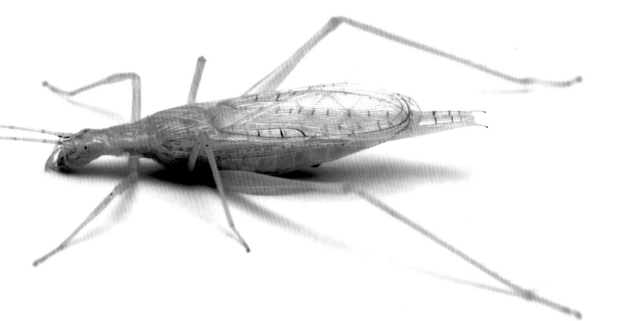

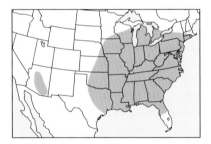

Arboreal in habits, the pale and lovely Davis's Tree Cricket resides high in trees and is difficult to find and collect, though well worth the effort. Violent thunderstorms may shake or knock them from their perches, and searching for them in the shrub layer after such a storm can be productive. Occasionally, a male can be found singing low enough to observe or capture with the help of a stepladder. In residential settings, this species is especially fond of dogwood trees. It was named after American entomologist William T. Davis (1862–1945).

Song: A mellow but rapid trill, irregularly interrupted by short pauses. The trill rate is about 65 pulses per second, given at a frequency of 2.5 kHz.

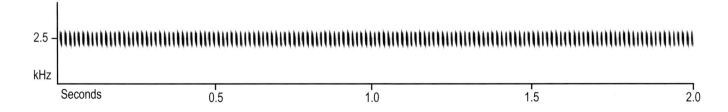

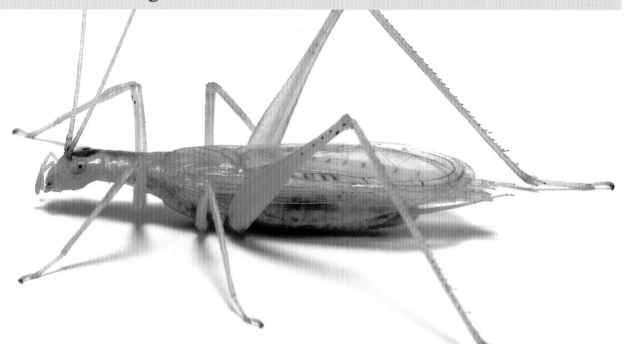

Light green in color with a prominent reddish cap, the Narrow-winged Tree Cricket is a handsome species that often sports pale blue eyes. Some individuals are particularly striking, with bright green veins on their wings. It frequents orchards, shrubbery, and gardens and may also be found in coarse weeds near the base of trees. Singing only at night, males are easy to locate and observe. They continue to sing even when illuminated with a light.

Song: A mellow trill of variable length, usually lasting about two to ten seconds, and sometimes with a slight sputter at the beginning or the end. Songs are separated by several seconds of silence. Pulse rate is about 65 per second, with a frequency of 3 kHz. This species and the Two-spotted Tree Cricket (page 76) are the only tree crickets in our area that typically sing trills of short duration.

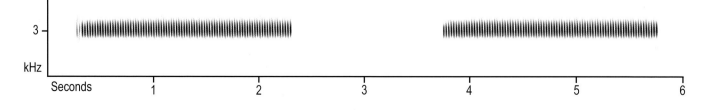

19. Two-spotted Tree Cricket *Neoxabea bipunctata* (1/2"–2/3")

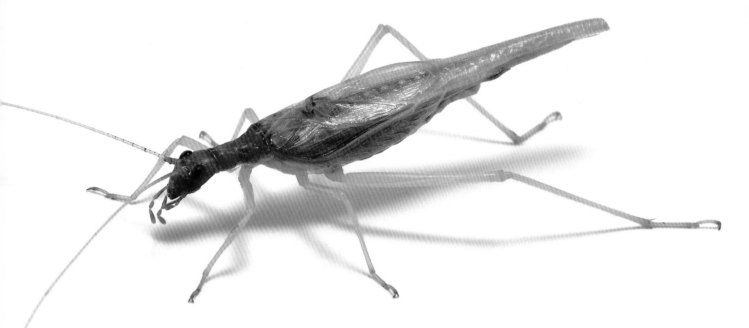

The Two-spotted Tree Cricket is an arboreal species attracted to dense vegetation, especially thick stands of young trees, where males sing from the underside of broad leaves. It generally stays well off the ground, making it difficult to observe or collect. This is the largest tree cricket in our area, however, and they can be plentiful. It is easily recognized by its reddish body with tan wings and legs. The common name is derived from the fact that females usually have two prominent dark spots on their wings.

Song: A plaintive, dissonant, buzzy trill at about 3.5 kHz, with a distinctive pulsing quality. The pulse rate is about 110 per second. Trills may be continuous, but they are usually marked by brief pauses occurring every few seconds or so. Trills are sometimes preceded by stuttering notes. During mating, the male produces a series of high-pitched clicks and scrapes that sound nothing like their typical song.

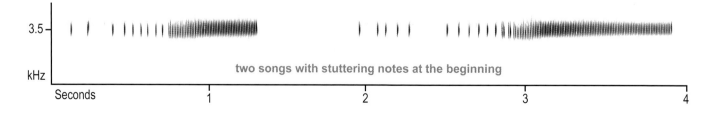

two songs with stuttering notes at the beginning

female with ovipositor

Mole Crickets
Neocurtilla and *Scapteriscus*

Aptly named because of their molelike body plan, the clumsy-looking mole crickets have enlarged forelegs adapted for digging. Not surprisingly, they spend the majority of their lives underground, where they dig extensive tunnel systems (although many species are capable of flight). Mole crickets may reach 2 inches in length and can be frightening when encountered. But there is nothing to fear. They cannot bite and are harmless when held (the most they can do is try to dig their way out of your hand).

There are seven species of mole crickets in North America (north of Mexico), four of them introduced. We include profiles of two species in this book. The most widespread in our area is the Northern Mole Cricket *(Neocurtilla hexadactyla),* which ranges throughout the East. In the southern states, there are three species in the genus *Scapteriscus,* all of which are native to South America, and all of which were introduced here about one hundred years ago. The most wide-ranging is the Southern Mole

Cricket *(Scapteriscus borellii),* first appearing in Georgia in 1904, and now found in coastal plain habitats from North Carolina to Texas. While the Southern Mole Cricket is mostly carnivorous, the other two species of the genus (the Tawny and Short-winged Mole Crickets, *S. vicinus* and *S. abbreviatus*) feed on roots and leaves and are among the most destructive of all our Orthopterans, causing extensive damage to lawns, golf courses, and crops.

Male mole crickets sing from their burrows. Within the genus *Scapteriscus,* males of some species construct horn-shaped entrances to augment their songs and project them skyward. This would make little sense were it not for the fact that females of these species fly prior to mating and home in on calling males. Mating occurs inside the burrow. At least in the Northern Mole Cricket, matings occur in a tail-to-tail position with the male lying on his back. After mating, the pair begins to fight, and it is likely that the female ejects the male from his burrow, taking it over in order to lay her eggs.

Southern Mole Cricket

20. Northern Mole Cricket *Neocurtilla hexadactyla* (3/4″–11/4″)

Northern Mole Crickets inhabit the damp margins of ponds and streams. They live in burrows in soft ground and are elegantly suited for a subterranean lifestyle, with stubby front legs equipped with enlarged claws, specially suited for digging in soil and sand. Additional adaptations for life in tunnels include a streamlined body, short legs, and small wings. The diet of the Northern Mole Cricket consists primarily of small insects and other invertebrates, along with some organic debris and plant matter.

Northern Mole Cricket males apparently call from closed burrows, probably to reduce their vulnerability to predators such as parasitic wasps. Nonetheless, their chirping is clearly audible aboveground and it is easy to home in on the general location of a burrow.

About half of all females are flightless and must travel on the surface or through the burrow system to reach the calling male. Burrows are equipped with an escape tunnel that allows the occupant to flee if pursued by a predator. Females lay their eggs in small chambers within the burrows. After sealing off her chamber, the female remains in the burrow to defend the eggs. Capturing Northern Mole Crickets is a supreme challenge. With difficulty, they can be flushed from their burrows, or else collected in special pit traps designed to catch dispersing individuals.

Song: The song of the Northern Mole Cricket consists of repeated chirps, given at a rate of about two per second. Each chirp is actually a brief trill composed of about 8 pulses. The frequency of the song is quite low for an insect, about 2 kHz, making it the lowest-pitched singer of all our native crickets.

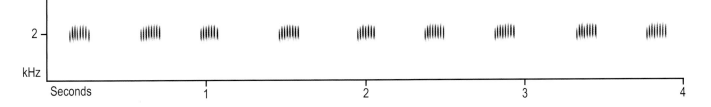

21. Southern Mole Cricket *Scapteriscus borellii (1")*

Native to South America, the Southern Mole Cricket and two other members of the same genus, the Tawny and Short-winged Mole Crickets, were introduced to the Southeast about a century ago, probably arriving as stowaways in the ballasts of ships. All three species are pests. The Southern, although primarily carnivorous, will eat the roots of newly planted seedlings in lawns and gardens, and the other two species, being mostly herbivorous, can cause serious damage to lawns, pastures, and golf courses.

Southern Mole Crickets make their burrows in wet sandy or mucky areas, often near streams, lakes, or ponds. Each evening before calling, males make and tune a special burrow that has a horn-shaped opening, allowing the male to amplify his song and direct it skyward. He sings mostly during the first two hours after sunset. Huge flights may occur during early evenings on warm spring days. Females find mates during these flights and are attracted to males with the loudest songs, landing near their burrows.

Song: A loud, continuous trill at about 3 kHz, given just after dark or after heavy rains. (Males also produce a special courtship song that resembles the song of the Northern Mole Cricket but is higher in pitch and delivered at a faster rate.)

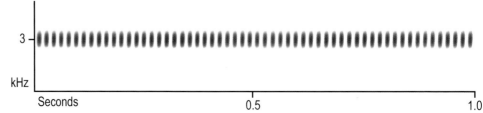

Trigs
Anaxipha, Cyrtoxipha, and *Phyllopalpus*

Also called sword-tailed crickets because of the sword-like shape of the female's ovipositor (see photo below), the trigs are a small group of tiny crickets that are easily overlooked, even though they may be numerous in their favored habitats. The word "trig" is entomological shorthand for Trigonidiinae, the taxonomic subfamily in which these crickets occur. There are eighteen species in North America (north of Mexico), represented by four genera. We include profiles for three species (in three genera) that are fairly common and widespread in the East.

Trigs range in color from reddish brown (Say's Trig) to bright yellow-green (Columbian Trig) and even a two-toned red-and-black (Handsome Trig). They inhabit brushy areas, shrubs, and trees, where males often sing while hiding under or between leaves. When disturbed, their small size helps them escape undetected. Males have trilling and chirping songs, and choruses can be surprisingly loud, in spite of the diminutive size of these noisemakers. Like tree crickets, male trigs hold their wings nearly straight up when they sing (see page 91).

Columbian Trig (female)

Handsome Trig

22. Say's Trig *Anaxipha exigua* (1/4″)

Small and delicate, the Say's Trig is a very handsome insect. This becomes more apparent if you inspect it with a magnifying lens and notice the head, which is decorated with a pattern of dark reddish brown bands set against light tan. Named after Thomas Say (1787–1834), who is often referred to as the father of American entomology, Say's Trigs are found in tall grassy areas along roads and in fields. Honey locust trees are a favorite haunt as well. To find them, look for locust tress in weedy, grassy areas and carefully inspect the branches. You may be surprised to discover hundreds of Say's Trigs residing in a single small tree.

Song: A clear, silvery trill at about 7 kHz that can be heard from a hundred or more feet away. The pulse rate is 35–40 per second. Males usually hide under a blade of grass when they sing. The song is so loud that it can be nearly impossible to locate the singer exactly, even when you're very close. Using a sweep net is the best method for collecting these minute singers.

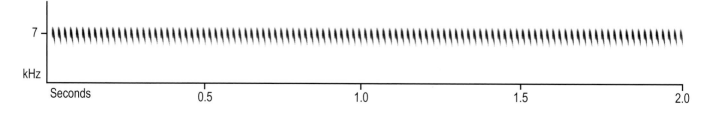

23. Columbian Trig *Cyrtoxipha columbiana* (1/4″–1/3″)

With its bright golden back, translucent green body, and eyes ranging from brilliant red to mottled brown, the Columbian Trig is quite stunning in appearance. Less than ½ inch long, individuals can be extremely difficult to locate, and a hand lens is required to see their unique beauty. Bradford pear trees as well as crape myrtle are favorite plants. Large colonies can often be found in one tree or bush while neighboring trees of the same species are empty. One way to collect Columbian Trigs is to place a sheet below a tree where they have been heard singing, then shake limbs and look for trigs that fall onto the sheet.

Song: A delightful, pulsating series of musical chirps that can be heard only from close by. Males in a colony roughly synchronize their songs, creating a steady, musical throb, reminiscent of distant sleigh bells. Each chirp is composed of about 5 pulses, given at a frequency of 7 kHz.

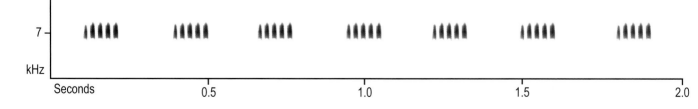

female

24. Handsome Trig *Phyllopalpus pulchellus* (1/4″–1/3″)

The Handsome Trig is certainly striking, with a black body, red head and thorax, and cream-colored legs with small patches of pure white accenting the bottom edge of the thorax and the legs. The Latin name for this species means "beautiful leaf-feeler." A more appropriate name could not be found. The mouthparts, or palps, are in constant motion—the trigs use them to "taste" their environment. Their antennae are also in perpetual motion, and the effect of the palps and the antennae whipping around is mesmerizing. Trigs are found in brushy hedgerows, especially thickets of Japanese honeysuckle.

Song: A rattling broken trill, pitched at about 7 kHz. Extremely loud for such a tiny insect. A male often sings from a perch where two leaves are very close together, making a chamber for his concert, which acts like a small megaphone to project the sound away from a bush or tree. The male holds his wings nearly straight up as he sings. His left wing is clear in the center. In prime habitats where there are large numbers, the chorus of trigs can be overwhelming.

immature

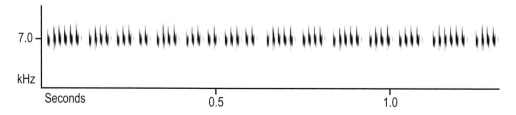

7.0 –

kHz

Seconds   0.5   1.0

Meadow Katydids
Conocephalus and *Orchelimum*

The meadow katydids (long-horned grasshoppers) are a familiar group. They are the little green grasshoppers with long filamentous antennae that frequent open, grassy areas. There are thirty-nine species in North America (north of Mexico), and nearly all of them fall into two groups: the small to medium meadow katydids (genus *Conocephalus*) and the large meadow katydids (genus *Orchelimum*). In this guide, we introduce thirteen common and widespread species, with examples from both genera. The meadow katydid clan includes some of our most colorful katydids, with bright green bodies complemented by shades of blue, yellow, red, and orange that cover the legs, eyes, or wings. Some species, such as the Handsome Meadow Katydid, are stunning in appearance, with rich translucent colors of surprising intensity.

Abundant in grassy meadows and other open areas, meadow katydids sound off with vigor when it's sunny and warm, but the high-pitched songs of the males are unmusical and quite unlike the pretty chirps and trills of crickets. Composed of soft ticks accompanied by swishy buzzes, rattles, shuffles, or purrs, meadow katydid songs are reminiscent of the rhythmic sounds made by a shaker full of rice or sand, or the high swishing of a drummer's brush against a cymbal. Though their songs are unmusical, a meadow full of katydids fiddling their tunes on a warm summer's afternoon can be quite pleasing to the ear, as if the grasses and weeds have joined together in a whispering chorus of pastoral tranquillity and joy.

With practice, the different species can be recognized by their songs. Each has a unique pattern, but confusion can arise because song tempo responds to the ambient temperature, just as it does in crickets and other katydids—when the temperature drops, everything slows down. Thus, a hot male of a species with a slow-tempo song might sound similar to a cold male of a species with a more rapid-tempo song. Males of each species can also be differentiated by their reproductive organs, in this case the cerci that extend from the rear of their abdomens. The diagram on page 95 presents drawings of cerci of the species included in this guide.

Short-winged Meadow Katydid

cerci

Drawings Showing Cerci of Male Meadow Katydids*

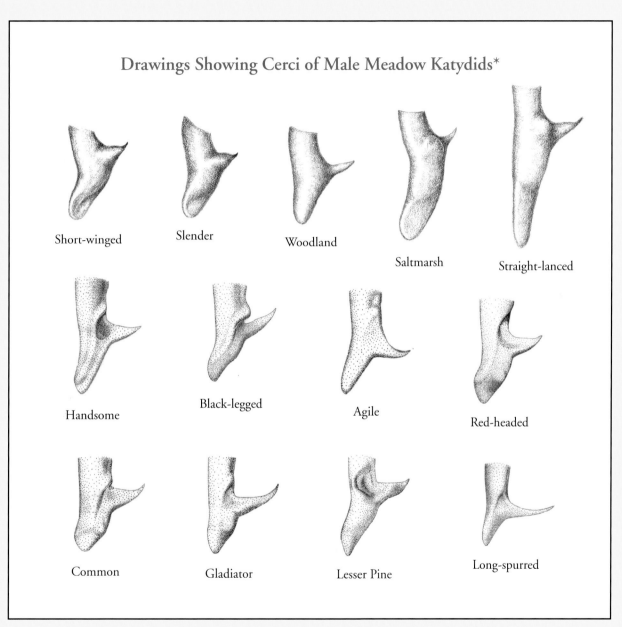

Short-winged

Slender

Woodland

Saltmarsh

Straight-lanced

Handsome

Black-legged

Agile

Red-headed

Common

Gladiator

Lesser Pine

Long-spurred

*Drawings by Susan Winewriter and Eliza Karpook, used with permission of the University of Florida.

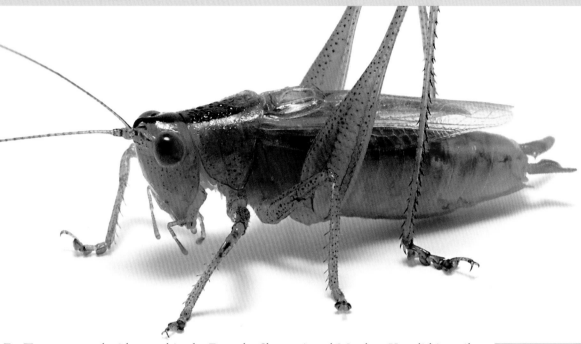

Numerous and widespread in the East, the Short-winged Meadow Katydid is easily overlooked because of its small size and its faint, high-pitched song. It is recognized by its bright green body, yellow-orange rear, and a dark brown band that runs from the top of its head back to its wings. Most individuals have short wings (but note the long-winged male on the facing page). It is found in areas of coarse weeds, grassy fields, and roadsides, in dry or wet areas. When approached, an individual will stretch out along the underside of a blade of grass, making it very difficult to spot. Easily disturbed, Short-winged Meadow Katydids are very good jumpers, making them difficult to catch.

Song: Song is composed of one to five ticks followed by a faint buzz lasting several seconds. Extremely high-pitched, with most of the sound energy from 10 to 20 kHz. Sings both day and night. Although the song is loud, it is so high-pitched that many people cannot hear it, even up close.

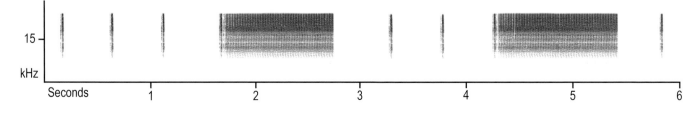

long-winged male

short-winged male

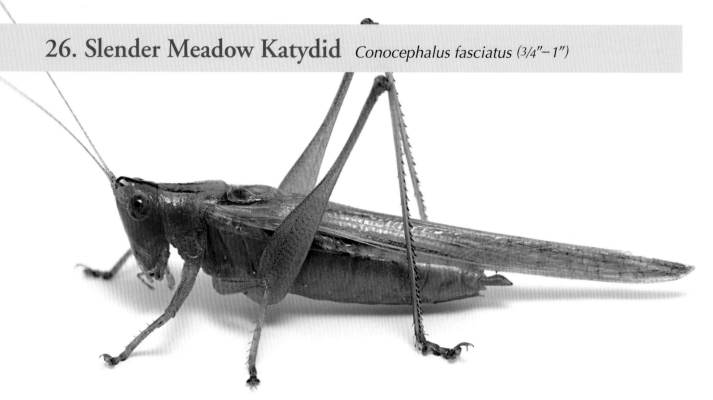

26. Slender Meadow Katydid *Conocephalus fasciatus* (3/4″–1″)

Named for its appearance, the Slender Meadow Katydid has long and narrow wings that extend well beyond its posterior. Its coat is a striking combination of green and brown. The species is broadly distributed but found very locally, seemingly in colonies. There appears to be a decline in body size across the country, with the smallest forms in the Northeast and the largest in the Southwest. To actually find a singing male by homing in on his faint, high-pitched song is a challenge. Quiet, warm, sunny afternoons are the best time to attempt this. Males are more easily collected by using an insect sweep net in areas of tall grass.

Song: An evenly spaced series of clicks or *tsips* followed by a faint, clicking purr or trill, at a frequency of 10–20 kHz. Song is pleasing to the ear, but difficult to hear because it is exceedingly high and soft.

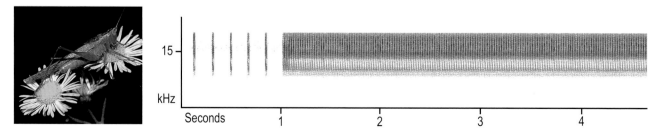

For those who study the Woodland Meadow Katydid, adjectives such as robust, rugged, and hardy all come to mind. Camouflaged by a coat of green, brown, and black, these katydids are hard to locate on dark vegetation. There are several color variations, ranging from near-black to tan or light green. They prefer areas of coarse weeds with saplings and forest nearby and are sometimes found sitting on twigs of deciduous plants in full sun. When disturbed, an individual will jump several times and then dig into the leaf litter, making capture difficult. A very hardy species; males can often be found singing from tree branches on warm sunny days well after the first snow.

Song: A series of brief, quiet buzzes or trills, often given at uneven intervals and sometimes preceded by a burst of rapid clicks. Peak frequency is 10–20 kHz. Song is pleasing to the ear.

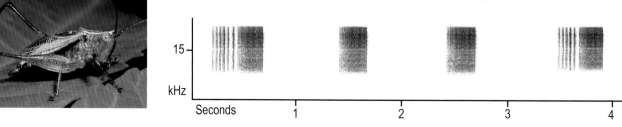

Perhaps the nicest-looking member of the genus *Conocephalus*, the Saltmarsh Meadow Katydid is a stunning combination of bright green, yellow, orange, and brown, with eyes colored a deep wine red. There is also an all-brown form. Found in saltmarshes along the coast from Maine to Texas, they prefer areas dominated by short grasses and reeds. Their song is faint, making them difficult to find. They are also great jumpers and are hard to catch, even with a net.

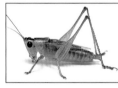

Song: An extended, clicking whirr at around 15–20 kHz that is difficult to hear, except at close range. A male will stop singing at the slightest disturbance and may wait several minutes before singing again.

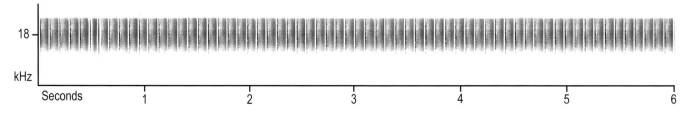

18 –

kHz

Seconds 1 2 3 4 5 6

29. Straight-lanced Meadow Katydid *Conocephalus strictus* (1/2″–1″)

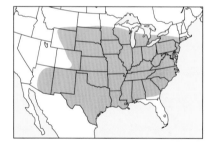

Named for the shape of the female's ovipositor (not pictured), the Straight-lanced Meadow Katydid is large, long-bodied, and dark in color compared to other small meadow katydids (see photo on page 94). They may occur in large numbers, but distribution is patchy within their range. The preferred habitat is open areas of short grass along roadsides and in pastures. Males have the peculiar ability to bend their bodies at odd angles. It is interesting to watch their interactions and movements; they are the contortionists of the katydid world.

Song: A faint, continuous purr at 10–20 kHz, often with a pulsating quality. Difficult to hear, but in a dense colony the combined sounds of individuals in a chorus can be impressively loud, even overwhelming.

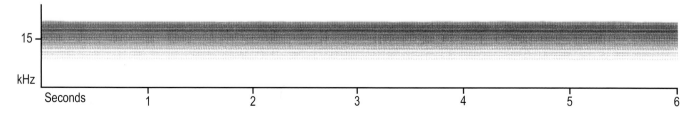

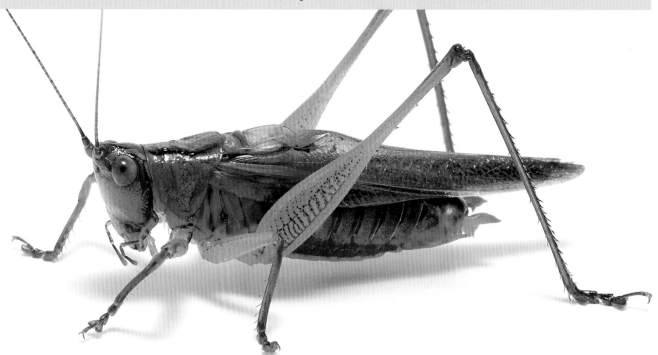

The Handsome Meadow Katydid is striking to behold, just as its common name implies. With bluish eyes, a pale face with red markings, vibrant green and turquoise on the body and wings, legs that are light yellow near the body and dark reddish brown toward the feet—this is one gorgeous insect. Found primarily in coastal plain habitats from New Jersey to Mississippi, it prefers damp areas with tall grasses, coarse weeds, and woody vegetation.

Song: A rapid burst of ticks followed by a loud, buzzy trill, extending from 5 to 20 kHz. Easy to hear. Large numbers of males are present in optimal habitat, and their cacophony can overwhelm the listener. When disturbed, most of the males in an area will immediately stop singing and hide by moving behind their perch. Sings both day and night.

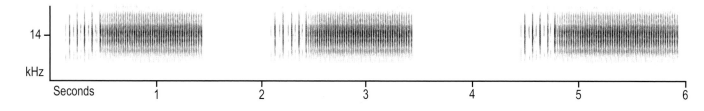

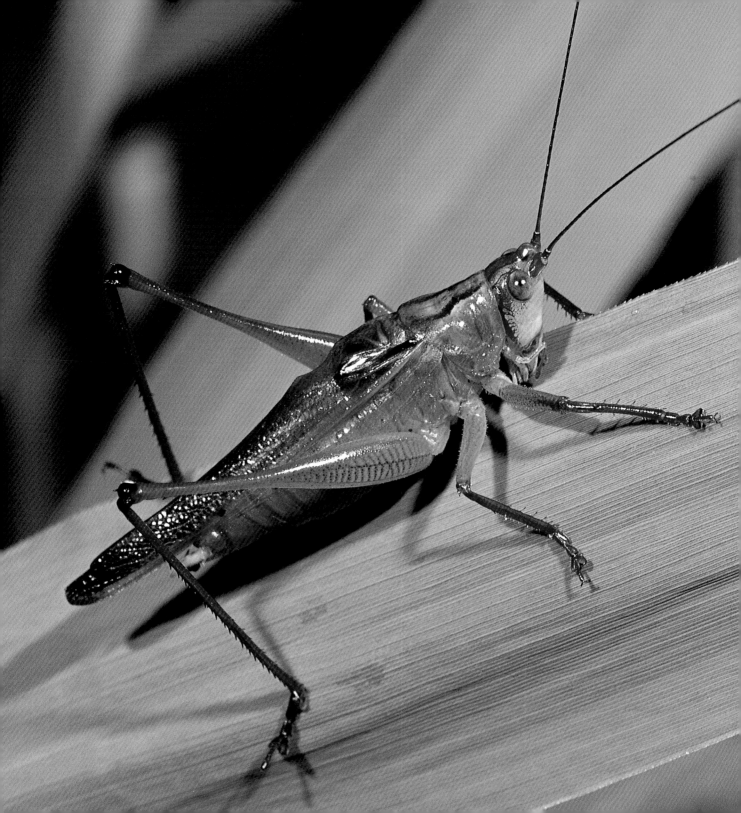

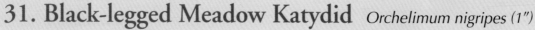

31. Black-legged Meadow Katydid *Orchelimum nigripes (1")*

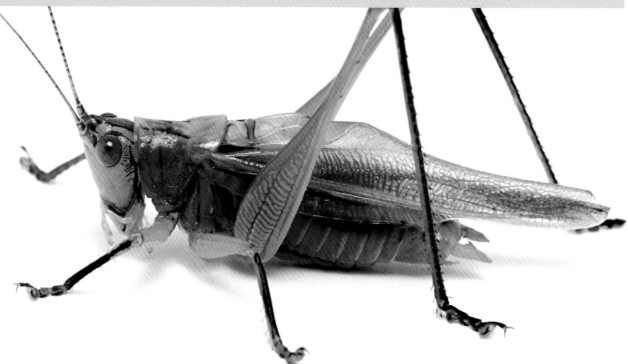

One of the prettiest members of its genus, the Black-legged Meadow Katydid sports a splendid combination of colors, with a blue-green body, red eyes, pale face, black legs, and bright yellow cerci. It favors grassy areas along the edges of wetlands and cattail marshes. Males sing from grasses and weeds and from the lower branches of associated shrubs and trees. Closely related to the Handsome Meadow Katydid (page 106), the Black-legged is found primarily west of the Appalachian Mountains.

Song: Several ticks followed by a loud, harsh buzz or trill at 10–20 kHz. Easy to hear. Sometimes ticks are given in an irregular series, without trills. Sings both day and night.

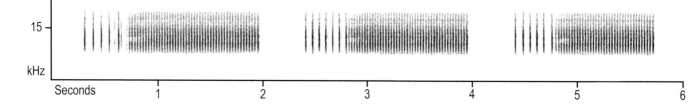

32. Agile Meadow Katydid *Orchelimum agile* (7/8″–11/8″)

With its muted green body set against creamy wings and head, the Agile Meadow Katydid is a subtly attractive member of its genus. It prefers open weedy and grassy areas that receive lots of sun. As the common name implies, these katydids are fast and agile. When approached, they first hide by moving to the far side of a stem or leaf. When further threatened, they will quickly jump several times before finally stopping to rest. Even when captured, their sudden, swift movements make them tough to keep in a net or cage.

Song: A rapid series of ticks followed by a dry, buzzy trill of variable length at 8–20 kHz. Loud and easily heard. May give lots of ticks without trills. Sings both day and night.

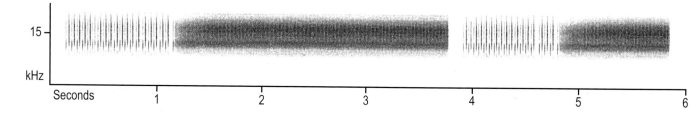

33. Red-headed Meadow Katydid *Orchelimum erythrocephalum (1″–1½″)*

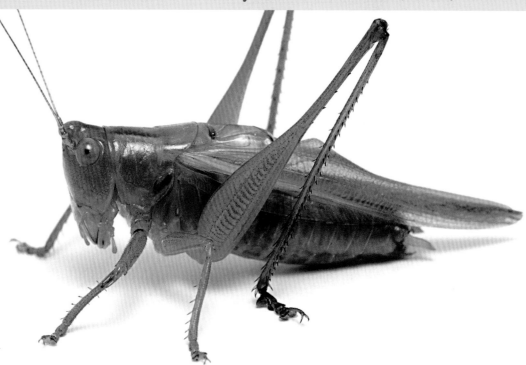

The Red-headed Meadow Katydid is large and stunningly handsome, with a variably bright red or orange-red head, and eyes ranging from black to pink or blue. They can be amazingly numerous in their preferred habitats, which can vary from inland palmetto thickets to seaside dune grasses. Even though abundant, they are often difficult to locate because singing males tend to stay hidden on the bottom side of leaves and stems, giving their song a ventriloquial quality.

Song: A loud staccato tick followed by a short buzzy trill at a frequency of 8–20 kHz. The singing pattern is distinctive, with songs given one after the other without pause, droning on uninterrupted to the point of almost being annoying. A long series of the ticks (without buzzes) may also be given.

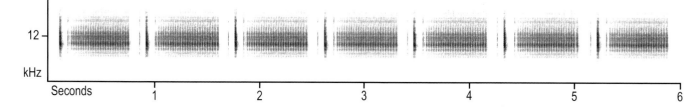

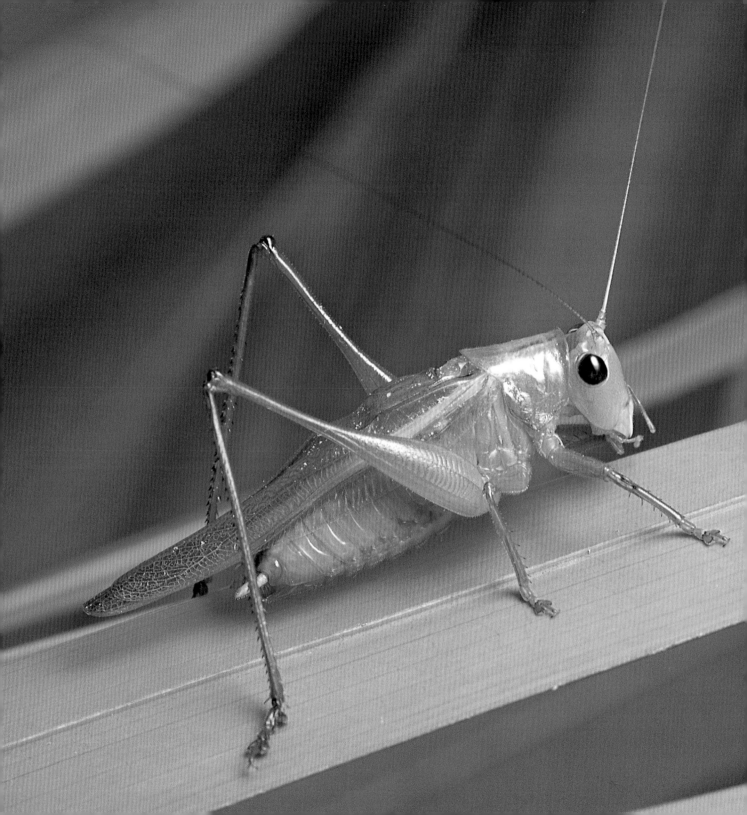

Not nearly as common as its name implies, the Common Meadow Katydid can sometimes be found in tall grassy or weedy patches along roads or along the edges of open fields. This robust species is easily caught because they typically do not hide when approached. It is very similar in appearance to its close relative, the Gladiator Meadow Katydid (page 116).

Song: A long series of ticks followed by a dry buzz that starts soft and quickly becomes louder. The frequency range is 10–20 kHz. Sings both day and night.

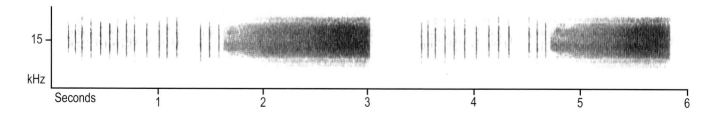

35. Gladiator Meadow Katydid   *Orchelimum gladiator* (7/8″–11/8″)

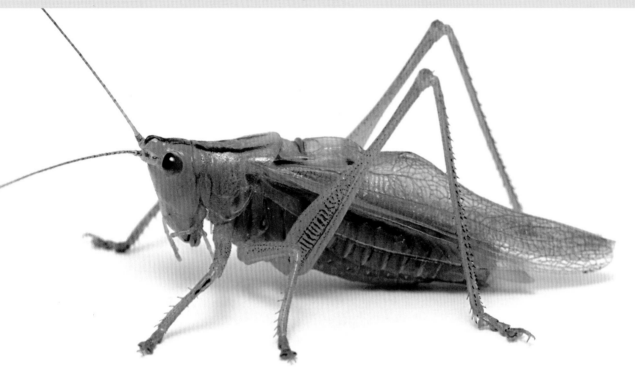

Built like a warrior, the stocky and stout Gladiator Meadow Katydid is aptly named. Its bright green body is accented with reddish eyes, brown on the back, and bright yellow cerci. Certain populations exhibit varying amounts of dark speckling on the sides of the body and legs. This common and widespread species inhabits tall grassy areas, often near water.

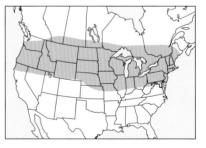

Song: A series of ticks followed by a long shuffling trill that starts soft and quickly gains in volume. Frequency is 10–20 kHz. In areas with dense populations, choruses have a unique wavering quality.

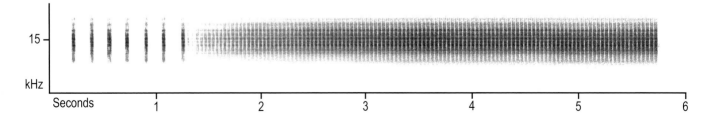

grooming male

female with ovipositor

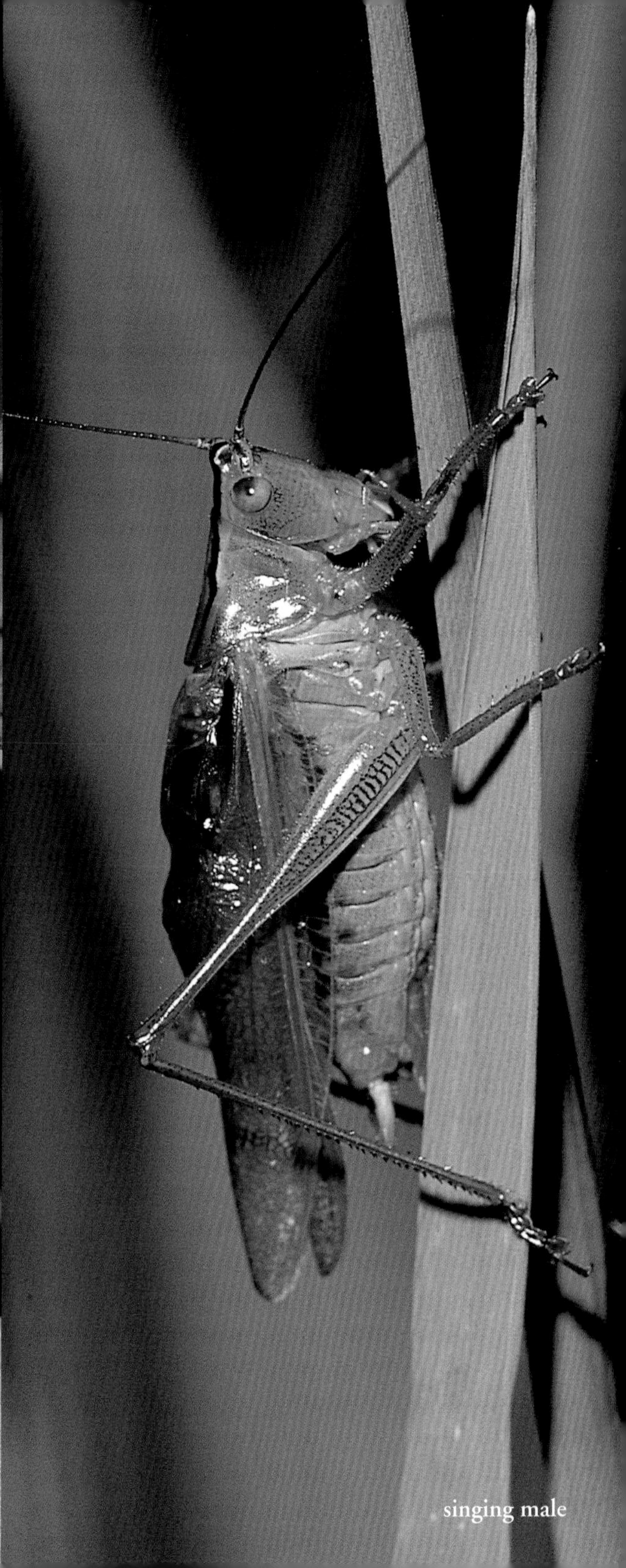

singing male

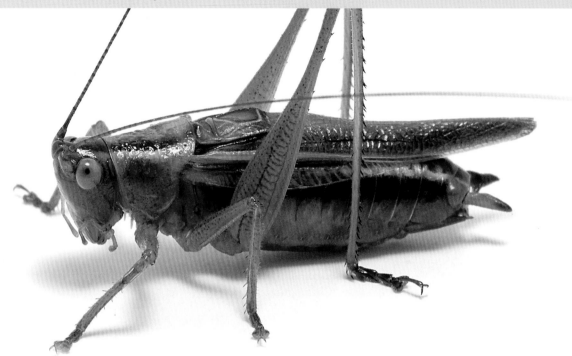

An inhabitant of pine trees and other evergreens, the Lesser Pine Katydid blends in so well that a singing male can be very difficult to find. Although camouflaged when resting on needles or cones, pine katydids are actually very beautiful, with orange eyes and legs, spruce green bodies, reddish brown backs, and yellow accents on their abdomens.

Song: An evenly spaced series of high-pitched shuffling trills, each lasting about a second. The frequency is 10–20 kHz. Song has a purring quality that makes it one of the most pleasing of all the meadow katydids, but many people have trouble hearing it. On a quiet afternoon in a pine thicket, the shuffles of pine katydids combine to create a blanket of restful sound, coming from all directions.

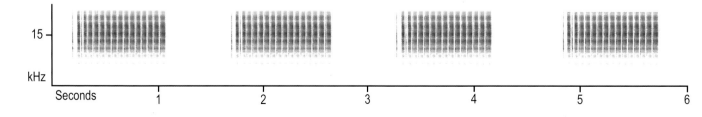

Bright orange eyes, a deep green body, reddish brown along the top of the abdomen, and yellow cerci combine to make the Long-spurred Meadow Katydid an elegant-looking member of its genus. This midwestern species is arboreal in habits and is fond of junipers and cedars. Named for the long spurs on its cerci, it is similar in appearance to its close relative, the Lesser Pine Katydid (page 118).

Song: Several seconds of loud stuttering ticks that blend into a long shuffling trill, with a frequency of 8–20 kHz. Listening to a colony spinning their songs on a warm summer afternoon is a pleasing and relaxing experience.

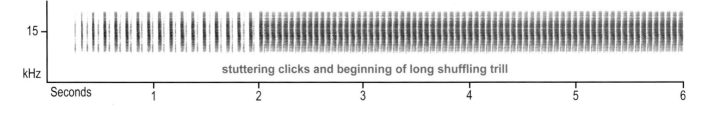

stuttering clicks and beginning of long shuffling trill

15 —

kHz

Seconds   1   2   3   4   5   6

Conehead Katydids
Neoconocephalus

Easily recognized by their slanted faces and pointed or rounded cones that extend from their foreheads, the conehead katydids look like insect battering-rams, ready to poke holes in whatever gets in their way. (Actually, scientists do not know the adaptive significance of the cones.) Coneheads have long and slender wings, and most are strong fliers. While some species are only an inch long, others grow to nearly 3 inches in length, ranking them among the longest of our native katydids. Nearly all species occur in two color phases, green and brown, with proportions of the two color phases varying widely between species. This variation in color has not been carefully studied, but it is thought to be adaptive, perhaps making it more difficult for predators, such as birds, to develop a stable search image of their prey.

There are twenty-two species of coneheads in North America (north of Mexico), represented by four genera. While most are eastern in distribution, a number are confined to the Southeast, and some are found only in southern Florida. In this guide, we feature five species of the genus *Neoconocephalus*, all of which are fairly common and widespread. Inhabiting tall grassy areas, weedy fields, and shrubby edges, male coneheads sing mostly at night and have loud raspy or buzzy songs. They are easy to find and catch but do not make good pets, because their songs are too loud and penetrating. The best way to identify a conehead is to look closely at the shape of its cone and note the pattern of dark coloration when it occurs. The opposite page has diagrams showing the undersides of the cones of the species included in this book.

Robust Conehead

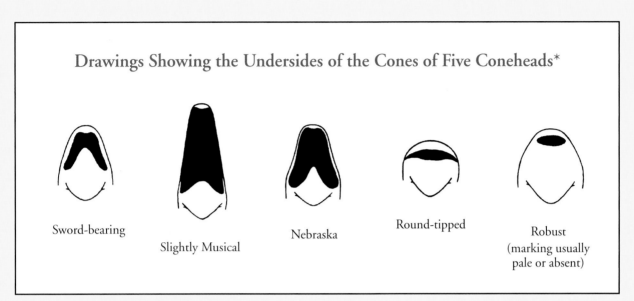

Drawings Showing the Undersides of the Cones of Five Coneheads*

Sword-bearing

Slightly Musical

Nebraska

Round-tipped

Robust
(marking usually
pale or absent)

*Drawings made from artwork provided by Thomas J. Walker.

Slightly Musical Conehead

38. Sword-bearing Conehead *Neoconocephalus ensiger* (1 3/4″–2 1/2″)

Impressive in appearance, the Sword-bearing Conehead is named for the extremely long ovipositor of the female, which can be nearly as long as her abdomen (see photo below). The cone is black on the bottom, with a light stripe wrapping around the tip. Look for these coneheads in weedy fields and tall grass along roadsides, particularly where there is some water nearby. When plentiful, green and brown forms can be found in nearly equal numbers. Brown individuals are peppered with dark spots on their wings—a very attractive effect.

Song: A rapid train of brief raspy notes at about 12 kHz, given at a rate of five to ten notes per second, depending on the temperature: *tst-tst-tst-tst-tst-tst* . . . Song is very loud and easily heard as one drives along country roads in late

female with sword-shaped ovipositor

summer or early autumn. Starts singing at dusk and continues throughout the night unless temperatures drop too low. Males often sing in unison on cooler nights. When disturbed, Sword-bearing Coneheads can react in a variety of ways. They may just sit still, or else move to the opposite side of the stem. Or they may suddenly fall headfirst into the vegetation and remain motionless and well hidden. In open areas, they often escape by taking flight.

13 —

kHz

Seconds   1   2   3   4   5   6

39. Slightly Musical Conehead *Neoconocephalus exiliscanorus (2″–2½″)*

Formerly called Long-beaked Conehead, the Slightly Musical Conehead has the longest head adornment of all. Its cone is black beneath, with a small hooklike crevice on the underside. This elegant-looking species is found in a variety of habitats, ranging from wetlands to cornfields, but in all situations it requires an abundance of water. Green and brown morphs occur in most populations. It is considered by some scientists to be an indicator species for wetlands—if it is missing from a wetland within its range, there may be a problem with the ecological health of that habitat.

Song: A spirited series of bright raspy buzzes that have a "slightly musical" quality, at least when compared to other conehead songs: *zee-zee-zee-zee-zee* . . . Song peaks at around 12 kHz and is given at a rate of about three buzzes per second. All of the males in a particular area sing in unison, creating a hypnotic nocturne that is pleasing to the ear.

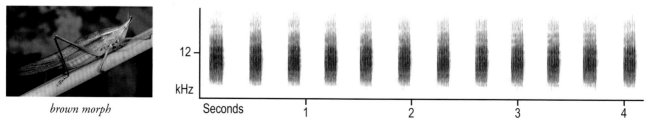

brown morph

12 -

kHz

Seconds   1   2   3   4

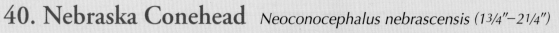

40. Nebraska Conehead *Neoconocephalus nebrascensis (1¾"–2¼")*

The Nebraska Conehead is perhaps not very well named. Yes, it is found in Nebraska, but its range is much broader, extending southward to Mississippi and eastward to Maryland. It occurs in both green and brown forms and is identified by its compact body structure, a broad head cone that is completely black when viewed from below, and wings that are unmarked or else lightly speckled with dark spots. Found hanging head down more often than not, an individual is prepared to execute its escape strategy—falling headfirst into the grass litter, where it will remain motionless to avoid detection. If fur-

ther disturbed, it will scurry away, work its way up a grass stem, and then fly away. Nebraska Coneheads are found along roadsides, in coarse weeds at the edge of fields and woods, and in brushy ground cover in open woods.

view of underside of cone

Song: A series of shrill buzzes pitched at around 10 kHz, each lasting one and a half to two seconds, with pauses of about one second between: *zeeeee . . . zeeeee . . . zeeeee . . .* Loud and piercing, song is both annoying and intriguing. Singing goes on continuously unless the male is disturbed. Neighboring males often synchronize their buzzes, with individuals starting at slightly different times but always stopping at exactly the same time, thereby accentuating the pauses between songs.

10 —

kHz

Seconds   1   2   3   4   5   6

41. Round-tipped Conehead *Neoconocephalus retusus (1½"–2")*

The smallest member of the conehead group, the Round-tipped Conehead has a petite cone that is very rounded and marked with a black line across the front. Found along roadsides and in pastures, it occurs in both brown and green forms. These coneheads are heard long before they are seen and are among the last coneheads to begin singing in the autumn. Easily approached and captured, they are not bothered by a flashlight. While they keep well in captivity, the song is not pleasant.

view of underside of cone

Song: A continuous, dry, raspy buzz at around 14 kHz, with a crackling quality that sounds like an electronic short. Sings in late afternoon as well as at night.

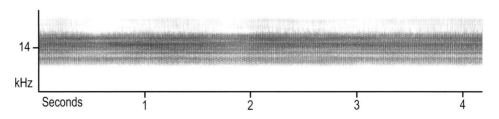

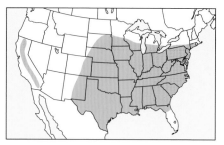

As its name implies, the Robust Conehead is the largest of the coneheads. Its rounded cone often contains no black areas and is accented with a yellowish stripe that wraps around the tip. Most individuals are yellow-green, but a brown morph also occurs. They are found in tall weeds along roadsides and in moist upland fields and along the edges of various wetland habitats. Driving country roads at night, you will have no trouble hearing this species—the song is so loud that you can hear it from inside a closed moving car.

Song: A continuous harsh buzz of incredible volume, with a peak frequency of about 8 kHz. Can be heard more than a thousand feet away! At close range, it becomes painful to listen to. One would think that the insect would burst into flames from the friction produced in creating such an intense song.

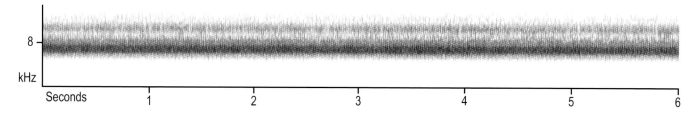

True Katydids
Pterophylla

The term "katydid" originated in North America. When early Americans beheld the raucous *ch-ch-ch* of Common True Katydids *(Pterophylla camellifolia),* they were compelled to make the sound part of their folklore. Several tales continue to circulate and our favorite goes like this: There was a woman named Katy who fell in love with a handsome young man, but she was scorned, and the man married another. Soon after, the couple was found dead, poisoned in their beds. No person saw what happened, but perhaps the bugs were watching, and on hot summer nights, they shout from the trees and tell us who-dunnit: *katy-did, katy-did, katy-did!*

The true katydids are an extremely diverse group, with over one thousand species found worldwide. Yet only four species are found in North America (north of Mexico), represented by three genera. Of these, the Common True Katydid—the quintessential noisy katydid with which most of us are familiar—is the only wide-ranging species in the East, and the only species covered in this guide.

The Common True Katydid is built like a tank, with cupped wings that give it a formidable appearance. Although they do not bite, they often squawk loudly when handled, puffing themselves up by pumping air between their forewings and abdomen. Their wings are well developed, but true katydids are apparently unable to fly. At most, when disturbed, they may leap from a leafy perch and flutter to the ground, where they walk to nearby tree trunks and climb back into the canopy.

Although they spend most of their life high in trees, they often gather in dense choruses during the breeding season, and individuals may sometimes be encountered walking across roads as they move toward noisy congregations. Rarely do males call from shrubs or small trees.

Females lay eggs in crevices in the bark or in soft plant tissue. The eggs hatch in the spring, and the nymphs feed on foliage until they reach adulthood, most never leaving the shelter of the canopy, and possibly the tree in which they were born.

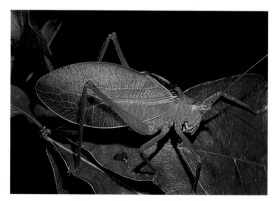

Common True Katydid (male)

Common True Katydid (female)

Our only representative of the genus *Pterophylla,* the Common True Katydid (formerly called Northern True Katydid) is the insect that everyone associates with the name "katydid." This species is large, bright green, and bulky in appearance. Even though its forewings are large, the Common True Katydid is incapable of flight. The males have a dark brown stridulatory field. It is extremely difficult to capture these katydids because they are usually high up in trees, especially oaks, and they blend well with their surroundings. During the breeding season, however, they may sometimes be found walking across roads, moving in the direction of dense choruses.

stridulatory organ of male

Song: One of the loudest among our native katydids—the forewings of males bow out slightly to create a resonance chamber that intensifies their calls. Songs are composed of harsh broadband notes that are loudest at 3–5 kHz but extend all the way to 20 kHz and beyond. Songs are given from dusk into the night, with males singing from perches high in deciduous or coniferous trees. They often form huge choruses, their combined songs drowning out nearly all other sounds. When there are many males in a location, each joins one or the other of two singing groups. Males within each group synchronize their songs while

female with ovipositor

the two groups alternate their songs, thus creating a resounding pulsation of sound that can overwhelm the listener. The night choruses of katydids actually frightened early Pilgrims, who had never experienced such sounds. When temperatures drop, males sing more slowly, with songs taking on a creaking or groaning quality.

There are three different populations or subspecies (indicated by different colors in the range map), each having a different calling pattern. Across the northern half of the range, katydids sing songs usually comprised of 2–3 harsh pulses delivered at a leisurely rate: *ch-ch . . . ch-ch-ch . . . ch-ch-ch . . .* (often likened to the words *ka-ty* or *ka-ty-did*). In the southeastern portion of the range, songs are comprised of 3–5 pulses that are delivered more rapidly, making each song sound like a brief rattle. In the southwestern part of the range, individuals sing slowly, with only 1–2 pulses comprising each song. The sonagram below depicts songs from the northern population.

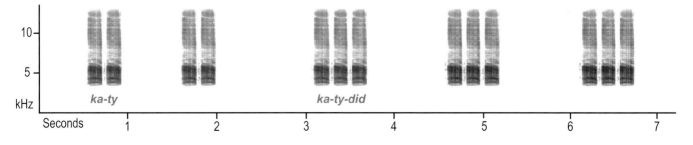

False Katydids
Amblycorypha, Microcentrum, and *Scudderia*

Ranging in color from bright yellow-green to deep leaf green, the false katydids are well camouflaged when perched on the leaves of trees, shrubs, and tall weeds. There is really nothing overtly "false" about this diverse group—entomologists simply refer to them this way in order to distinguish them from the true katydids, which belong to a different taxon. There are about sixty-five species of false katydids in North America (north of Mexico), represented by twelve genera. Many of these are western species, and a number have very limited distributions. In this book, we feature twelve species in three genera and include nearly all the common species in the East. The three groups covered are the round-headed katydids (genus *Amblycorypha*), the anglewings (genus *Microcentrum*), and the bush katydids (genus *Scudderia*).

Not surprisingly, the round-headed katydids have rounded heads (see photo on opposite page). Most species are bright yellow-green in color, and some are decorated with a scattering of small dark spots, as if someone sprinkled them with a dab of pepper. Delicate in appearance and full of personality, some make excellent pets. The songs of males range from simple swishy rattles or clicks to complex sequences of sounds. In fact, the song of the Common Virtuoso Katydid is one of the most complicated and outstanding of all our insect musicians.

With intricately patterned ridges and veins on their angled forewings, the leaf green anglewings are unrivaled leaf mimics (see photo below). Anglewings are widespread and common in their preferred habitats but are difficult to track down because males typically give their ticks, *zits,* and rattles from high in trees. Instead, look for them on window screens and porches, drawn at night by the lights.

As a group, the bush katydids have angular features and are more slender and lean than our other katydids. Many are quite elegant in appearance, arrayed in gorgeous shades of green and yellow. Found from forests to meadows, the males have songs that range from simple ticks or shuffles to pleasingly intricate sequences of buzzes. There is even one that appears to count when it sings (see page 162). In most species, the males sing intermittently, and their sounds have a ventriloquial quality that makes them difficult to find.

Bush katydids tend to look alike, and the key to identifying males by sight is the shape of their tail plates, as shown in the diagram on page 140. It is also notable that male bush katydids produce sperm packets that are accompanied by a large, edible gelatinous mass. After mating, the female consumes this "nuptial meal" while the contents of the male's sperm packet are emptied into her (see photo on page 21).

Lesser Anglewing Katydid

VISUAL IDENTIFICATION OF BUSH KATYDIDS

Bush katydids of the genus *Scudderia* look much alike, especially to the novice. While some can be recognized by their general appearance or possibly by the shape of their wings (such as the Broad-winged Bush Katydid), the best way to identify males is to look carefully at the reproductive structures at the rear of the abdomen. Pay particular attention to the shape and size of a male's tail plate, when viewed from above.

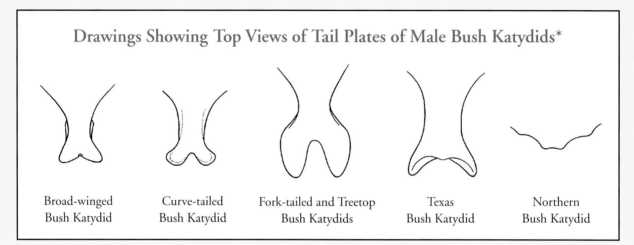

Drawings Showing Top Views of Tail Plates of Male Bush Katydids*

| Broad-winged Bush Katydid | Curve-tailed Bush Katydid | Fork-tailed and Treetop Bush Katydids | Texas Bush Katydid | Northern Bush Katydid |

*Drawings from J. A. G. Rehn and M. Hebard. 1914. Studies in Tettigoniidae: 1. A synopsis of the species of the genus Scudderia. *Trans. Am. Entomol. Soc.* 40: 271–314.

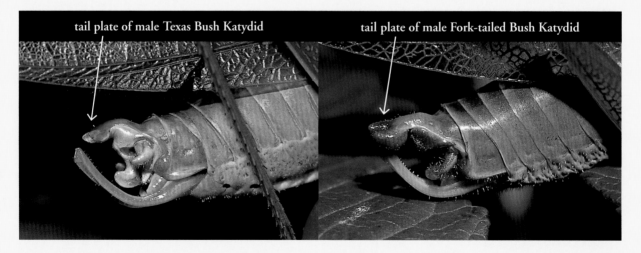

tail plate of male Texas Bush Katydid   tail plate of male Fork-tailed Bush Katydid

Broad-winged Bush Katydid

44. Rattler Round-winged Katydid *Amblycorypha rotundifolia* (1⅛″–1½″)

Abundant though seldom seen, the bright green Rattler Round-winged Katydid is an excellent leaf mimic. Moving about slowly and deliberately, these katydids are difficult to locate, even when one is singing right in front of you. Unusual color morphs, such as the amazing pink specimen pictured below, are rarely encountered. This species seems loaded with personality; when confronted, one will turn and look at you as if to say, "What do you think you're doing?" They rarely fly. When disturbed, they weakly jump away. Females are more bluish than the males, and they have a prominent upturned, serrated ovipositor. Adults are very susceptible to frosts and do not survive the first couple of freezing nights. This species is found along the edges of woods in brushy vegetation and in second-growth habitats.

Song: A high-pitched swishy rattle with a frequency of around 12 kHz. Often gives a song series consisting of ten to twenty brief rattles lasting about one second each followed by a long terminal rattle.

rare pink color morph

several brief rattles followed by beginning of an extended terminal rattle

12 —

kHz

Seconds 1   2   3   4   5   6   7   8

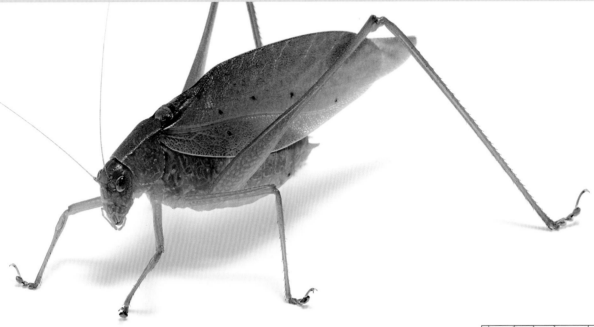

45. Clicker Round-winged Katydid *Amblycorypha alexanderi (1⅛"–1½")*

With an appearance nearly identical to the Rattler Round-winged Katydid, the Clicker Round-winged Katydid can be identified by its unique clicking song. Found in the understory of deciduous woodlands, these endearing little katydids are docile and slow moving. Yet, when encountered, they act unconcerned and seem to project an attitude that they are fully in charge. The wings may or may not have spots. This species, along with several other small amblycoryphids of similar appearance, have received a great deal of study recently, resulting in the description of several entirely new species.

Song: A measured series of raspy high-pitched clicks or *zits,* delivered at a rate of three to four per second. The peak frequency is about 12 kHz. A click-series typically lasts about five to ten seconds, followed by several seconds of silence, then another series of clicks.

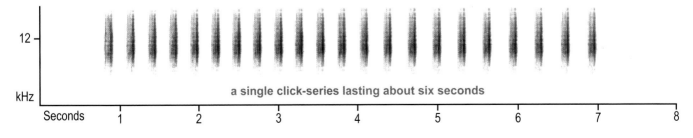

a single click-series lasting about six seconds

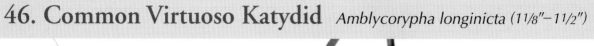

46. Common Virtuoso Katydid *Amblycorypha longinicta* (1⅛″–1½″)

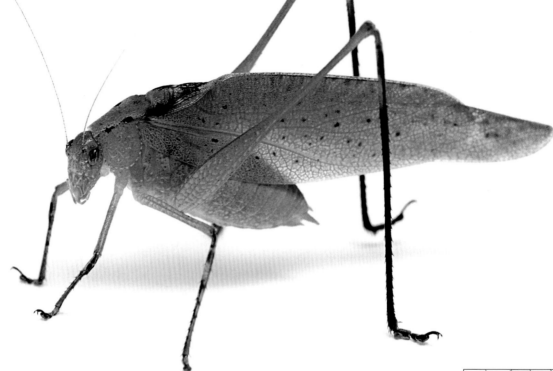

Virtuoso is certainly an appropriate name for this gorgeous katydid with an exceptional song. Built on the same basic plan as other members of the genus *Amblycorypha,* the Common Virtuoso Katydid can be recognized by the brown coloration of the lower portions of all its legs, as well as the scattering of dark spots on its back and wings. What's more, the Virtuoso's complex song is perhaps the most amazing of all the Orthopterans.

Song: Highly variable from one individual to the next but composed of several distinct kinds of sounds. Because of its complexity, it is difficult to say exactly where a song begins or ends. Nevertheless, song may unfold as follows: Every few seconds or so we may hear a brief shuffle that drops in volume from beginning to end. Then we may hear a series of ten or more sharp ticks, given at a rate of one or two per second. Then we might hear a few more brief shuffles. Then comes the most remarkable utterance: a three-part rattling sequence that lasts five to ten seconds and gradually builds in volume like a musical crescendo. Sequences typically begin with raspy shuffles that grade into a series of rattling ticks that get louder and louder before suddenly terminating with an accented shuffle. Song is quite loud, but with a peak frequency of around 15 kHz, it can be difficult to hear.

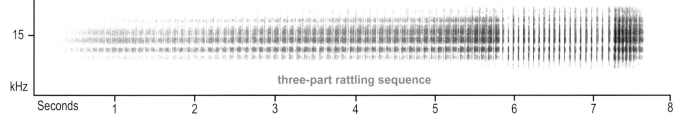

three-part rattling sequence

15 kHz

Seconds 1 2 3 4 5 6 7 8

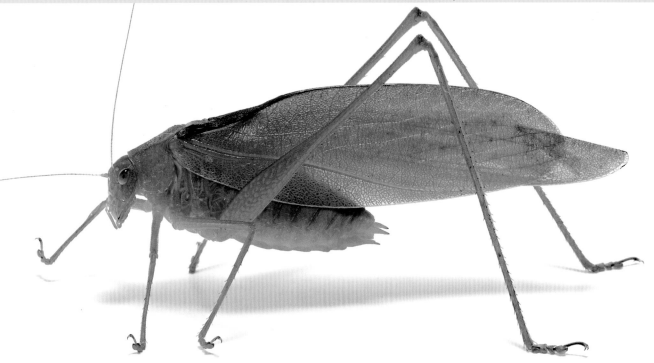

The largest member of its genus, the Oblong-winged Katydid can be recognized by its very dark stridulatory field and wings that extend farther back from the body than on other amblycoryphids. Oblong-winged Katydids are powerful fliers and can easily escape a collector. They prefer open weedy habitats with tall vegetation, where they perch near the tops of plants to sing. They also like apple orchards. Very rarely, pink or yellow individuals may be found within a dense population (see photos below).

Song: A brief, two-parted *zeee-dik!* at around 9 kHz, given every few seconds. This unique song is easily distinguished from the songs of all other katydids.

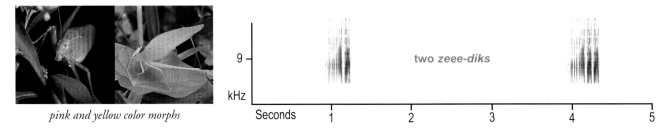

pink and yellow color morphs

two *zeee-diks*

9

kHz

Seconds   1   2   3   4   5

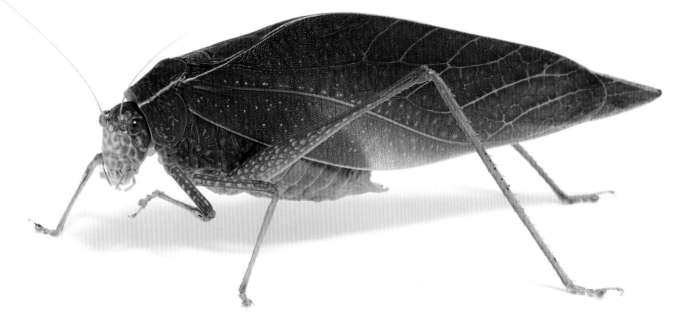

A stunning leaf mimic that has to be seen to be appreciated, the Greater Anglewing can be identified by its green stridulatory field (the Lesser Anglewing has a brown field). The intricate pattern of veins on the wings perfectly imitate the appearance of a leaf. This species is difficult to collect because it perches in the tops of trees and tall bushes. Sometimes, however, one can be found low enough to catch. It may be very common in rural backyards, where its high-pitched ticks betray its presence.

Song: The male has two types of songs. A staccato *dzt!* (pitched at around 9 kHz) may be given every few seconds. This song causes receptive females to approach the singing male. The second song type is a rapid series of high-pitched ticks, lasting several seconds. If a receptive female is nearby, she will give an answering tick, allowing the male to home in on her in order to mate.

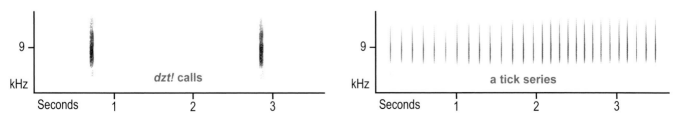

49. Lesser Anglewing *Microcentrum retinerve* (1¾″–2″)

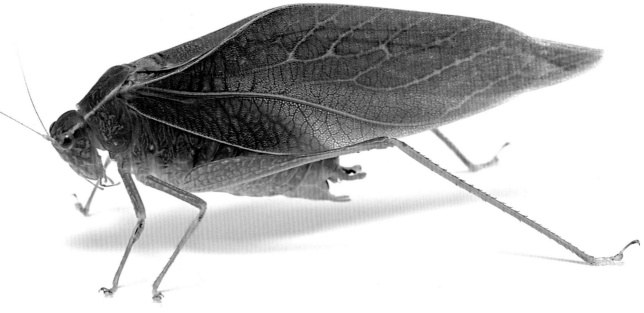

Another amazing leaf mimic is the Lesser Anglewing. Recognized by its brown stridulatory field, this species is smaller than the Greater Anglewing. It blends in so well that you can be looking straight at one and not see it. Like its cousin, the Lesser Anglewing usually sings from high in trees. However, males often perch at the ends of branches. Concentrating your efforts there will increase your likelihood of finding one of these extraordinary-looking insects.

Song: A brief raspy rattle, often produced in groups or two or three, with about a second of silence between each call. Each rattle is composed of 3–5 pulses, given just a little too fast to count. The time between song bouts can be very long. The peak frequency is 8–10 kHz.

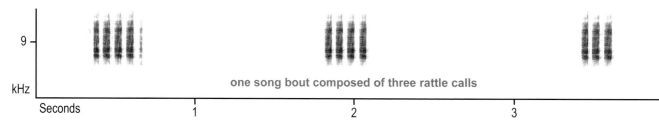

one song bout composed of three rattle calls

Named for the pronounced curvature of the female's ovipositor, the Curve-tailed Bush Katydid inhabits coarse weedy fields and weedy wood margins. It is particularly abundant in Michigan, Indiana, and Ohio, where males can be found singing from the tops of goldenrod plants.

Song: Consists of two to five raspy, buzzy notes given in quick succession that typically increase in volume: *zit-Zit-ZIT.* Sings intermittently, but often gives songs in pairs, usually with four or more seconds of silence between the two songs and the second song having one more pulse than the first (songs may also be given in groups of three). Sings both day and night, with most singing activity in the evening. Peak frequency of song is 8–9 kHz.

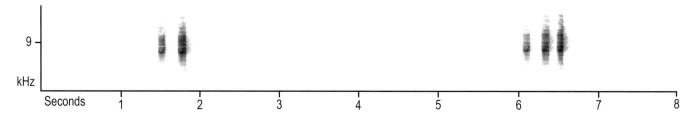

51. Texas Bush Katydid *Scudderia texensis (1⅝″–2¼″)*

Perhaps a misnomer, the Texas Bush Katydid is broadly distributed east of the Rocky Mountains. An elegant-looking katydid, its green body is often accented by varying amounts of purple or rufous on the legs and the abdominal segments. Late-season individuals, especially after a frost, can be rufous all over and may at first appear to be a different species. While it may be difficult to home in on a singing male, this species is easy to approach and capture.

Song: There are two principal song types that are given both day and night. The more common is a brief shuffling rattle made up of three or four lispy notes that are delivered too fast to count. A less common song pattern is a series of about fifteen lispy notes, given too fast to count, that rise in volume from beginning to end. The peak frequency of songs is about 12–14 kHz.

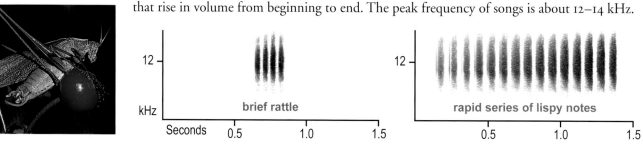

brief rattle

rapid series of lispy notes

The Fork-tailed Bush Katydid is a widespread species, ranging from coast to coast. In the East, it inhabits bushy areas, especially near woods. A male can be identified by its large brown or purplish dorsal processes, which are bifurcated and rounded with the appearance of a horseshoe. The female's ovipositor is also colored, with a deep brown or reddish tint. The male Fork-tailed's reproductive parts look almost identical to those of the Treetop Bush Katydid (see diagram on page 140), but the latter can be identified by its dark wing-edges (see page 160). Pink color morphs are common in certain Louisiana and Arkansas populations. The Fork-tailed is not an accomplished singer—its simple call occurs intermittently, and considerable patience is required to home in on a male, who is likely to be discovered near the end of a branch.

Song: A single sharp *tsip* that may be given singly, or else in a series of two or three, with a few seconds of silence between each call (a typical series of three

pink color morph (female)

female with ovipositor

is pictured in the sonagram). The dominant frequency is about 15 kHz. Especially during social encounters, the Fork-tailed may also give high-pitched ticks.

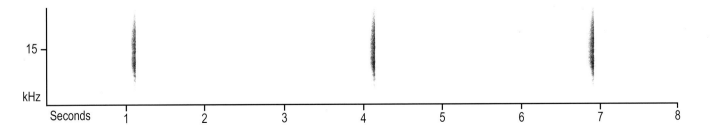

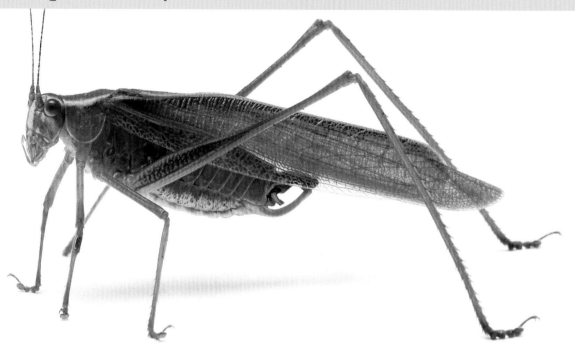

53. Treetop Bush Katydid *Scudderia fasciata* (1⅜″–1⅞″)

As its name implies, the Treetop Bush Katydid is an arboreal specialist. It prefers coniferous stands but may also be found in deciduous trees and shrubs. This gorgeous katydid has deep green upperparts and a striking pattern of purple and white on the underside of the abdomen. The upper edges of the forewings are accented with black, and the distal portions of the legs are tinged purple or dark brown. Treetop Bush Katydids are difficult to observe unless found in a patch of young trees where they are low enough to see.

Song: The most common song is a simple, abrupt *tsip* at about 15 kHz that sounds identical to the song of the Fork-tailed Bush Katydid. The two species are best told apart by comparing collected specimens. Another less common call is a grating *zzzit*.

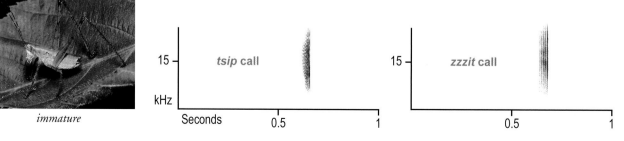

immature

tsip call

15 —

kHz

Seconds 0.5 1

zzzit call

15 —

0.5 1

54. Broad-winged Bush Katydid *Scudderia pistillata (13/8″–2″)*

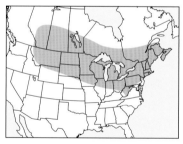

Elegant and regal are adjectives that might be applied to the Broad-winged Bush Katydid. It differs from other *Scudderia* in that the forewings are broad—the lower edge of each forewing curves down, making this katydid noticeably wider at the middle than other species in the genus. Common in upland meadows of goldenrod and asters but also found in damp areas and among high-bush blueberries, they are masters of camouflage. Even when singing from a few feet away, a male can be nearly impossible to spot. You can sometimes capture one by flushing it and following it to its new perch.

Song: A katydid that counts! The nocturnal song is a series of about five groups of lispy buzzing notes with a peak frequency of about 10 kHz. The male starts by giving a quick sequence of two or three buzzes. After remaining silent for a number of seconds, he next gives a rapid sequence of four or five buzzes. After another long pause, he gives a sequence of five or six buzzes, and so forth until he completes the entire series. In other words, each successive utterance in a song series adds one or two buzzes, as if the insect were counting. The interval between these "counting sequences" is highly variable but is usually a number of minutes. There is also a gradual increase in volume from the beginning of a series to the end. Broad-winged Bush Katydids sing a different song during the day—a five-syllabled lispy rattle, given singly or in a series.

female with ovipositor

10

kHz

a typical counting sequence going from a group of three buzzes to a final group of nine buzzes

Seconds 5 10 15 20

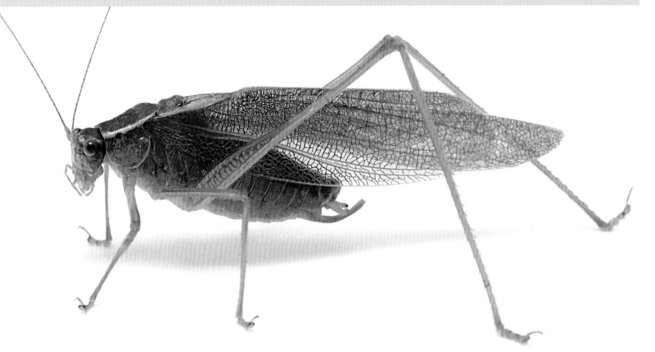

The first of the *Scudderia* katydids to sing during the summer, the Northern Bush Katydid prefers the tops of small trees or shrubs in open habitats or open woods. Difficult to capture because they are too high up, they are attracted to lights and may sometimes be collected near porch lights or on window screens at night.

Song: The most accomplished singer of the bush katydids. The very high-pitched song, given only at night, is a series of soft ticks followed by five to ten lispy buzzes that are given in quick succession and are usually followed by a series of very loud ticks. The dominant frequency of the buzzes is 12–15 kHz.

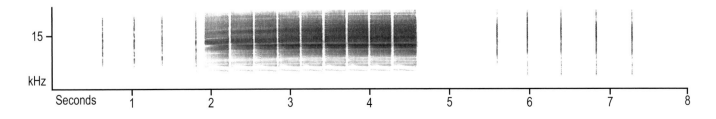

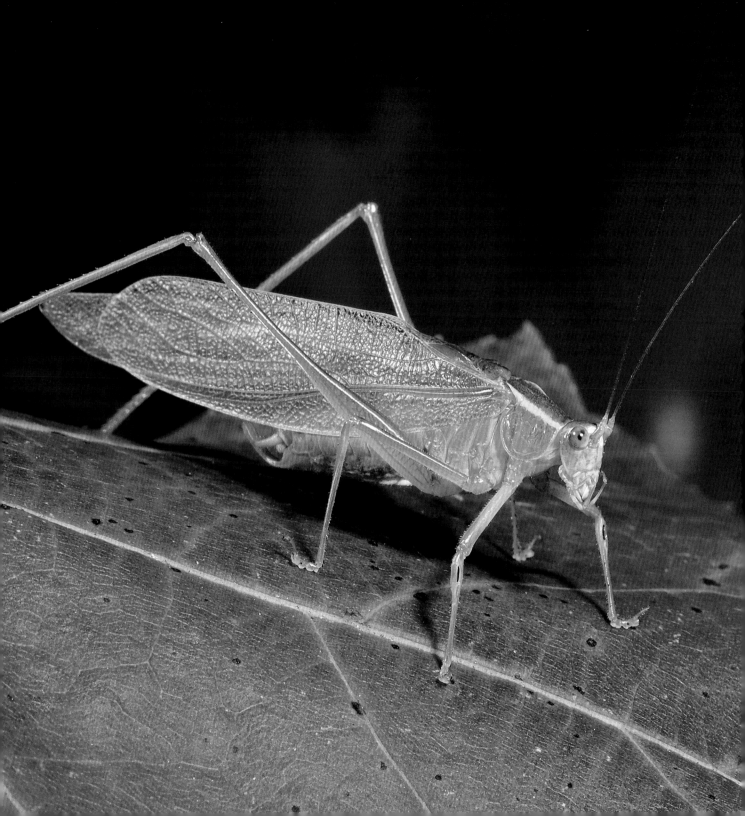

Shieldback Katydids
Atlanticus and *Metrioptera*

Named for the enlarged shieldlike plates that cover the tops of their thoraxes, the shieldback katydids are the linebackers of the katydid world, with robust bodies and a fierce demeanor (they may look mean, but like most katydids, they are harmless when handled). An extremely diverse group, there are 123 species of shieldbacks in North America (north of Mexico), represented by 25 genera. Nearly all are western in distribution—only 10 species occur in the East, most being members of the genus *Atlanticus* (eastern shieldbacks). In this guide, we feature four eastern shieldbacks, plus the Roesel's Katydid, a northeastern species in the genus *Metrioptera*.

The shieldbacks are usually the first katydids to emerge as adults. Males can be heard singing as early as mid- to late June, in weedy fields and brushy woodland understories. Species can be identified by the pattern of their high-pitched songs, which are swishy rattles or trills, difficult for many people to hear. Species also look different, showing variations in the length of the hind legs relative to the body and the length of the forewings protruding from the shield. Colors vary from neutral gray to reddish brown (note also the rare green color form of the Least Shieldback, pictured to the right, and the yellowish color variant of the American Shieldback, pictured below).

American Shieldback (yellowish color morph)

Least Shieldback (greenish color morph)

56. American Shieldback *Atlanticus americanus* (3/4″–11/8″)

Reddish brown in color, the American Shieldback has an elongated appearance. Its legs are longer than those of most other members of its genus (only the southeastern Robust Shieldback has longer legs), and its very short wings barely extend from below its shieldlike midsection. This species is found in wooded areas, where males sing from low vegetation or from the sides of trees. Once seen, they are easy to capture.

color variant

Song: A steady series of very high-pitched, swishing rattles. Each rattle lasts approximately half a second, with a quarter-of-a-second pause between. The male sings for about a minute, then is silent for about a minute, then sings again. Song has a very wide frequency range, with most energy concentrated around 15 kHz and above.

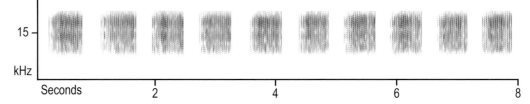

Protean Shieldbacks are among the most numerous of our native shieldbacks. Inhabiting weedy fields with scattered trees, they are among the first of the katydids to sing in early summer, beginning in June in the southern portions of their range. Males start singing from the leaf litter just before the sun goes down. As it gets dark, they gradually move up into trees or other tall vegetation and continue singing through the night. Protean Shieldbacks are easy to approach, but their habitats are typically dense, and reaching a singer can be exceedingly difficult, unless you're a professional contortionist.

Song: A dry, rattling trill with a pulsing quality that is given continuously, though broken at sporadic intervals by very brief pauses. The peak frequency is around 15 kHz. The pulsating quality of the Protean Shieldback's song is unique, and it allows for reliable identification of the species.

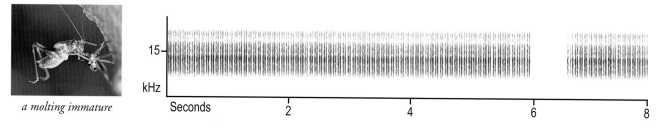

a molting immature

15

kHz

Seconds   2   4   6   8

58. Least Shieldback *Atlanticus monticola (3/4″)*

The Least Shieldback is a striking and robust katydid of weedy fields and brushy forest understory. Its pinkish brown coloration makes it one of the most attractive of the genus (note rare green color morph pictured on page 167). It can sometimes be found walking on

the trunks of trees at night, probably hunting for prey (shieldbacks are carnivorous and feed upon small invertebrates, including other insects). The Least Shieldback has well-developed forewings but no true hindwings. The forewings extend only a short distance down the abdomen. The abdomen is large and bulging—a fall from a height of a few feet can actually cause fatal injury if the abdominal wall ruptures. If disturbed, the Least Shieldback may suddenly jump away with the aid of its powerful hind legs.

singing male

Song: A long series of brief swishy rattles, given at a rate of about two per second, or else at uneven intervals. Sings at dusk and into the night. The rattles are very high-pitched and have a broad frequency spectrum, peaking at 15 kHz, which is

172

near the upper limits of human hearing. For this reason, many people cannot hear their songs. Adults begin singing in late June in the southern parts of the range and may be heard until the first hard frost.

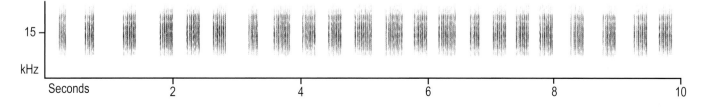

59. Robust Shieldback *Atlanticus gibbosus (1"–1⅓")*

The Robust Shieldback is perhaps the most elegant member of the genus *Atlanticus*. It is long and lean in comparison to other shieldbacks, and it is clothed in rich browns and salmon reds, typically accented by dark patches on the sides of its midsection. It is fairly common in sandy pine woods of the Southeast, where males sing from the ground or from low vegetation. Note that the forewings are almost completely hidden by the shield.

Song: A series of five to fifteen bright swishy rattles, delivered in a measured sequence. There are usually thirty seconds or so of silence between each song series. The peak energy of the song is around 15 kHz.

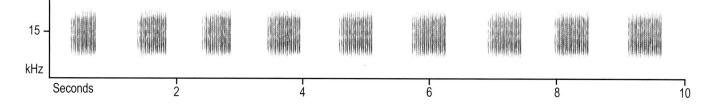

60. Roesel's Katydid *Metrioptera roeselii* (1/2″–3/4″)

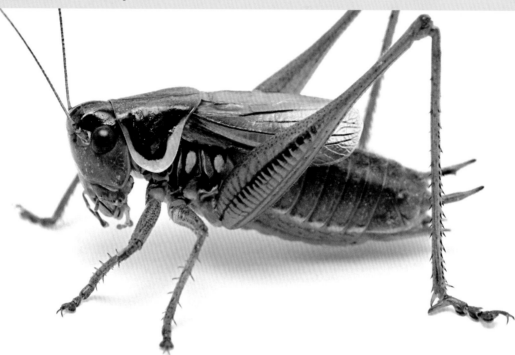

At first glance the colorful Roesel's Katydid looks like a short-horned grasshopper, but it is actually a member of the shieldback group. A European species, it was accidentally introduced to Montreal in the early 1950s and has since spread well into the United States. There is an isolated population in Illinois. Abundant in optimal habitat, the Roesel's Katydid prefers open, grassy areas. Males sing both day and night from the stems of grasses and weeds. Short-winged and long-winged forms occur.

Song: A high-pitched quavering buzz that may be given continuously or in a broken series. The peak frequency is about 15 kHz. Song has a crackling quality similar to an electronic short. At close range, it is hard on the ears.

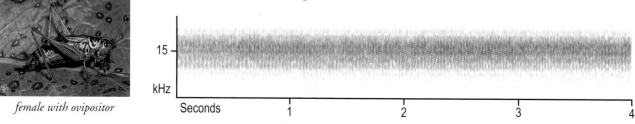

female with ovipositor

15 —

kHz

Seconds   1   2   3   4

singing male

Grasshoppers (Locusts)
Chorthippus, Dissosteira, and *Spharagemon*

Visit almost any weedy field, lawn, or dusty dirt road in the summertime, and you will encounter grasshoppers (locusts), familiar Orthopterans that can be distinguished from katydids by their short antennae or "horns" (some people refer to katydids as "long-horned grasshoppers" and the locusts as "short-horned grasshoppers"). Grasshoppers are ubiquitous in sunny habitats throughout our region, although they are usually absent or uncommon in northern areas and in wet swamps and marshes. Few species inhabit shaded forest, and those that do are generally found in small clearings that receive direct sunlight. Most grasshoppers are well camouflaged with coats of brown or green, but there are some rather colorful species (such as the well-known Eastern Lubber Grasshopper of the southeastern states).

There are over 650 species of grasshoppers in North America (north of Mexico), a huge number to be sure, and most of these are western in distribution. Unlike the noisy meadow katydids, the majority of grasshoppers do not stridulate. But there is one group, the slant-faced grasshoppers, that are known for their soft and muffled songs. Males of this group "fiddle their tunes" by rubbing the inner surface of their hind femurs against the edges of their forewings. Another group, the band-winged grasshoppers, make an entirely different kind of sound. Males, and sometimes females, make loud snapping or crackling sounds with their wings as they fly, especially during courtship flights. This unique mode of sound production is called "crepitation," the snapping sounds apparently being produced when the membranes between veins are suddenly popped taut (band-wings also stridulate, but their songs are typically weak and subtle). Because most grasshoppers do not make sounds, and those that do are difficult to hear, we have decided to feature only three species in this guide, including a common slant-faced grasshopper that stridulates (Marsh Meadow Grasshopper) and two band-winged grasshoppers that crepitate (Carolina and Boll's Grasshoppers).

Marsh Meadow Grasshopper

Carolina Grasshopper

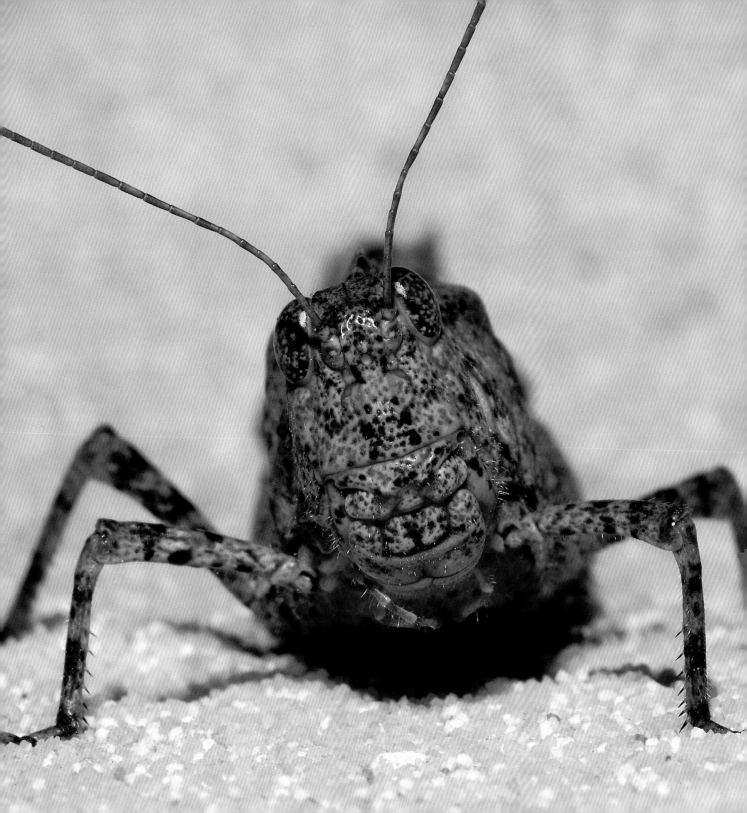

The Marsh Meadow Grasshopper is a member of the slant-faced grasshopper group (Gomphocerinae), which contains a number of species that stridulate. Individuals sound off by rubbing the inner surface of their hind femurs against the edges of the forewings, like the bow of a violin being pulled across a taut string. There are "stridulatory pegs" on the femur, which aid in sound production. A very widespread species, the Marsh Meadow Grasshopper inhabits moist areas of tall grasses. Both sexes stridulate.

Song: A rapid series of about thirty-five very high-pitched raspy notes, starting softly but quickly gaining in volume. Each song lasts about five seconds. The dominant frequency is around 16 kHz.

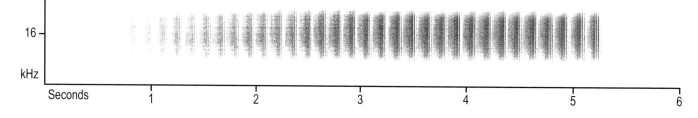

62. Boll's and Carolina Grassshoppers *Spharagemon bolli* and *Dissosteira carolina (1¼″–2¼″)*

Boll's Grasshopper — *Spharagemon bolli*

Common throughout the East, the Boll's and Carolina Grasshoppers, along with most other band-winged grasshoppers, inhabit dry areas. The Boll's Grasshopper prefers dry spots in open, sunny woods. The Carolina Grasshopper prefers barren sites and is often found on sunny dirt roads, in fallow fields, or in gravel or sand pits. With mottled coats varying in color from neutral gray to yellowish or reddish brown, both are well camouflaged when resting on the ground and are difficult to spot until they fly. If one is flushed, watch carefully where it lands, then approach slowly for a better view. These abundant species, along with most other band-wingeds, are very difficult to catch without persistent effort with an insect net.

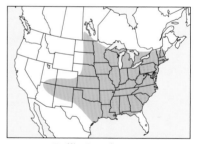

Boll's Grasshopper

Song: Males of both species commonly crepitate, producing a crackling series of snaps or clicks as they take flight, or as they hover or fly in a butterfly-like fashion during courtship. These sounds, which are auditory signals used in courtship, have a broad frequency range and are apparently made as a male pops taut membranes on his wings as he flies (males are able to fly without crepitating). Both species also stridulate while perched, as do many other band-wingeds, but their songs are weak and not often heard.

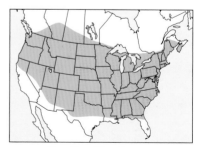

Carolina Grasshopper

Carolina Grasshopper — *Dissosteira carolina*

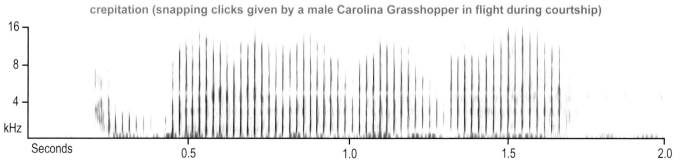

crepitation (snapping clicks given by a male Carolina Grasshopper in flight during courtship)

Cicadas

Tibicen, Okanagana, Neocicada, and *Magicicada*

Grotesque and frightening in appearance, cicadas do not bite and are actually harmless to handle. They are members of the order Homoptera, close relatives of the aphids and leafhoppers. Most cicadas, including all of our eastern species, are excellent fliers and spend their adult lives high in trees, where they are difficult to see. Some species, however, frequent city parks and woodlots, and injured specimens may sometimes be found along sidewalks or on window screens, or else cats may catch them and bring them home. Cicadas are also drawn to bright lights at night. Unlike crickets and katydids, which do well in captivity, cicadas usually die within several days and should not be kept as pets. While some cicadas can be recognized at a glance, others look very much alike and are best identified by their loud songs, which people notice, even if they don't know they're being made by cicadas. There are lots of cicadas in North America (north of Mexico), about 155 species represented by 14 genera, although most of these are western in distribution. We cover 13 species in this guide (in 4 genera) and include the common species most likely to be heard in the East.

The typical cicada life cycle lasts many years. Females generally lay eggs in the bark of limbs or twigs (see photo below). The eggs hatch into tiny nymphs that fall from trees and then burrow into the ground, where they feed on roots. The nymphs remain underground for a number of years, growing steadily and shedding numerous skins. Finally, they emerge from the ground, crawl up tree trunks, and then shed their last skins to become adults, leaving their nymphal cases attached to the bark (see photos on pages 22 and 206). Over most of our region, emergences begin in midsummer. Adults live only about a month, feeding on plant juices, which they obtain by inserting their piercing and sucking mouthparts into the bark (see opposite).

Male cicadas have loud buzzing songs that are produced by special organs called "tymbals," located on the first segment of the abdomen. Most species are easy to identify by song. A male's song attracts females and may also serve to attract other males, especially in those species that form noisy mating aggregations.

Nearly all of our eastern cicadas are of the annual type, meaning that adults emerge every year, although some years may yield greater numbers than others. In other words, the life cycles of individuals within a population are staggered, so that there are nymphs emerging as adults every year. In contrast, the "periodical" cicadas have populations in which all individuals are synchronized in their life cycles. The example we include in this book is Linnaeus's 17-year Cicada, in which individuals in a population emerge all together just once every seventeen years (see page 210 for more information).

Linnaeus's 17-year Cicada (cross section of stem showing eggs laid in bark)

Davis's Southeastern Dog-day Cicada (feeding)

sucking mouthparts
inserted into bark

63. Scissor-grinder Cicada *Tibicen pruinosa (1⁷/₈″–2″)*

Resembling the sound made when grinding scissors, the exaggerated pulsations of the Scissor-grinder Cicada's song make this species easy to identify. Found in deciduous woodlands throughout its range, it also commonly frequents suburban yards, orchards, and city woodlots. There are two disjunct populations of this species. The eastern population *(T. pruinosa winnemanna)* ranges from New York southward to Alabama, while the western population *(T. pruinosa pruinosa)* ranges from Michigan and Iowa southward to the Gulf of Mexico. Some scientists believe these are two distinct species, even though they sound alike. And to complicate matters, there is yet a third population in certain coastal areas that may also prove to be a new species.

Song: Loud and buzzy, with slow and pronounced pulsations at a rate of 1–2 per second. Lasts about twenty seconds, with a peak frequency of around 5 kHz. Begins soft, builds to a crescendo, then tapers off at the end. Males can be heard singing from late morning until dusk.

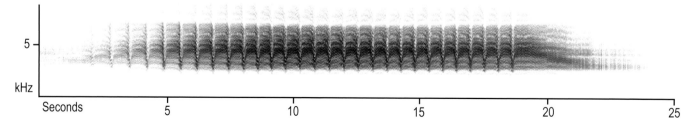

The Swamp Cicada is the only eastern species that is frequently found on low weedy vegetation and shrubs in swampy or marshy habitats, as well as in dry upland meadows and overgrown fields. Swamp Cicadas are dark-bodied, with bright green patches on their heads and prominent blue-green veins on their wings. It should perhaps be renamed "Morning Cicada" because of its striking habit of singing from early morning until noon, with very little singing in the afternoon.

Song: Begins with a soft buzz that gradually changes into a pulsating drone that increases in volume to a crescendo, and then gradually tapers off before ending abruptly. Song length is ten to fifteen seconds, with a peak frequency of around 6 kHz.

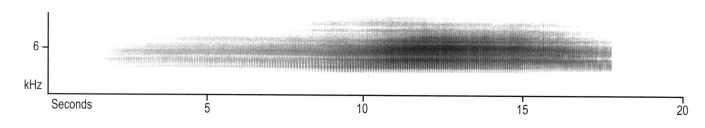

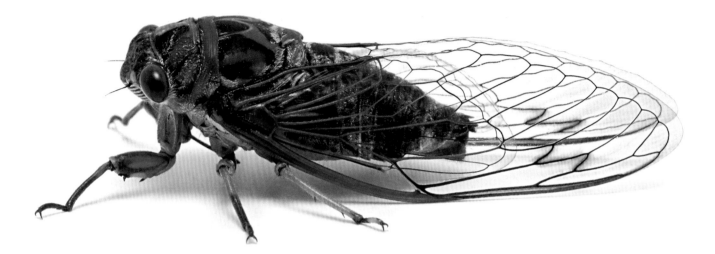

An inhabitant of deciduous forests throughout much of the East and Midwest, Linne's Cicada is often common in city woodlots and parks, where nymphs emerge from burrows at night in midsummer, climb the trunks of trees, and then pause to shed their skin. Newly emerged adults are a wonder to behold. Soft and delicate to touch, they appear translucent and are bright blue-green in color. There is a prominent bend along the lower edge of the wing that is distinctive. Once emerged, a young adult remains motionless for an hour or two as it dries its new exoskeleton, expands its wings, and darkens in color. If there are Linne's Cicadas in your town, look for this miracle of nature an hour or so after sunset on the first nights after you have heard males singing.

Song: High-pitched and rapidly pulsating. Begins softly but quickly increases in volume, then becomes a steady pulsating rattle sounding like a saltshaker, before ending abruptly. Sometimes continues to buzz softly between songs. Peak frequency is about 7 kHz and song length about fifteen seconds. Sings all day long during warm spells.

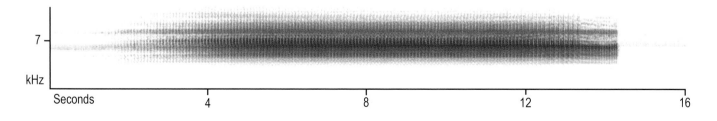

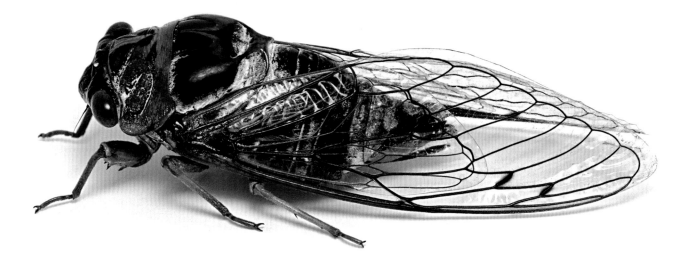

The largest of the eastern and central cicadas, the Northern Dusk-singing Cicada is black-bodied with dull green and brown accents and with portions of its body covered with cottony white material. It is found in nonmountainous eastern deciduous woodlands, where it sings from high in trees (individuals are occasionally found singing from low branches). Named for its habit of singing almost exclusively at dusk, this species is attracted to the glow of high-intensity sodium vapor lights; exhausted cicadas can often be found on the ground under the lights. Captives often emit a very loud alarm buzz, reminiscent of a fire alarm bell.

Song: A heavy pulsating drone lasting fifteen to twenty seconds, with a peak frequency of about 3 kHz: *drrr-drrr-drrr-drrr-drrr-drrr . . .* Often smooths out near the end, before tapering off and ending abruptly. Easily recognized by its low pitch in comparison to the songs of most other cicadas.

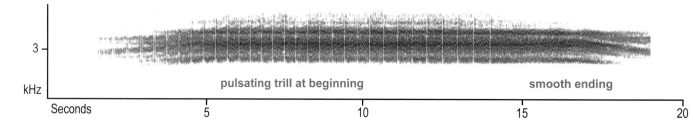

og-day Cicadas are widespread and vocal. Their brown and green markings are almost identical to those of Linne's Cicadas, but Dog-days are noticeably smaller in size. The common name comes from the fact that this species exhibits peak singing during the time of the year when the star Sirius, of the constellation Canis Major (the big dog), is prominent in the night sky. These typically hot and muggy days of July and August are referred to as the "dog days" of summer. The exact range of *Tibicen canicularis* is not well known, but it is the only cicada in northern areas that sounds like a buzz saw. It is often found on or around pine trees.

Song: A high-pitched whining drone that lasts about fifteen seconds. Starts soft, gets louder, then tapers off at the end. Reminds many of the penetrating buzz of an electric saw. Peak frequency is about 7 kHz.

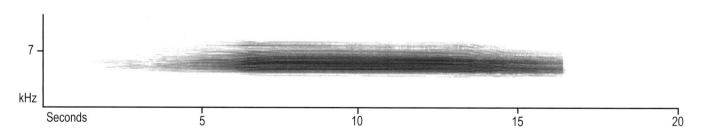

68. Davis's Southeastern Dog-day Cicada *Tibicen davisi (1¼″–1½″)*

An attractive small cicada with rich brown and green markings, the Davis's Southeastern Dog-day Cicada may be heard singing in coastal plain forests from New Jersey to Louisiana, from high in deciduous trees or pines.

Song: A whining buzz without pulsations that sounds very similar to the song of *Tibicen canicularis* (page 194), but with a much shorter duration of six to seven seconds. Song starts soft, gets louder, then tapers off at the end. The peak frequency is about 7 kHz. Over most of its range, the Davis's Southeastern Dog-day Cicada is the only species with a short "buzz saw" song that lacks the pulsations typical of many other cicadas.

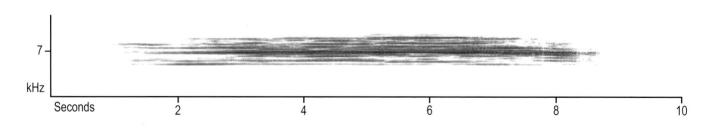

69. Lyric Cicada *Tibicen lyricen (1⅞"–2")*

The Lyric Cicada is variable in appearance, with some individuals sporting prominent red-brown patterns on their head and thorax, and others having just a touch of red-brown on the top of their head, usually in a T-shaped pattern. Preferred habitats include deciduous forests, wooded residential areas, and orchards. It sings all day long on warm days, but there is usually a peak in singing at dusk.

Song: A buzzy, rattling trill with a peak frequency of about 7 kHz, and lasting from thirty seconds to a minute or more. Lyric Cicada songs are fairly easy to identify because they do not have the pulsating character of the songs of most other cicadas in their range. Songs start soft, then increase in volume, and may exhibit distinct changes in volume before finally ending.

alternate color form

7

kHz

Seconds   10   20   30   40

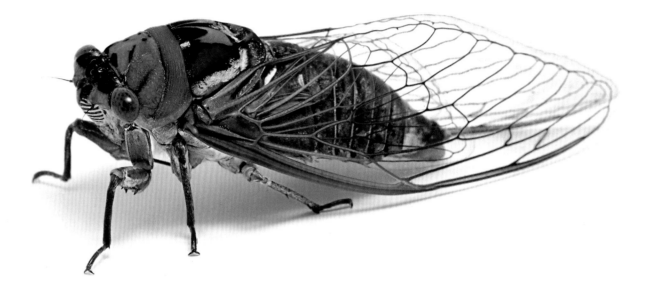

Colorful and striking in appearance, the robust and beautiful Walker's Cicada has green, rufous, and white markings on its head and thorax and blue-green veins at the base of its wings. It is fond of bottomland areas near rivers, where males sing from small trees and especially from willows. While it is easy to home in on a singer, he will prove difficult to collect because Walker's Cicadas are highly alert and agile fliers.

Song: An extended, dry, rattling trill or drone, with segments of prominent pulsations commonly alternating with segments of smooth trilling. This song is quite unlike the songs of other cicadas found in the same range. Peak frequency is about 6 kHz. Males in earshot of one another sometimes synchronize their singing.

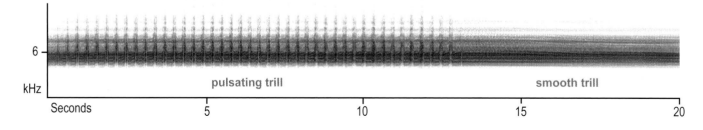

71. Robinson's Cicada *Tibicen robinsoniana* (1¾")

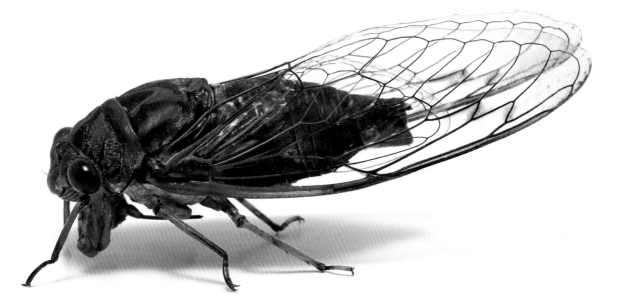

Robinson's Cicadas are dark-bodied with extensive brown or reddish brown markings (some individuals also have prominent green areas). This species has a patchy distribution and occurs in widely isolated populations (see range map). Males sing from the tops of deciduous trees, often along the edges of rivers, and are very difficult to collect. The singing period is short compared to that of most other cicadas—males typically quit singing after the first few cool nights in September.

Song: A laborious series of raspy buzzes, each lasting about one and a half seconds. Buzzes are given one right after the other, and a sequence may last several minutes or more. Heard mostly in the evenings on warm late summer days, but may sing all day long. Songs have a peak frequency of about 5 kHz.

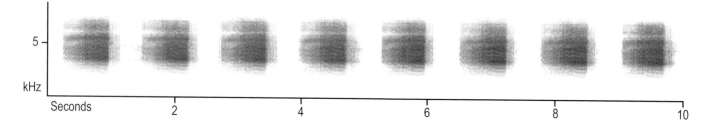

green form

brown form

An inhabitant of northern areas of limestone soils and white cedars (and other conifers), the dark-bodied Canadian Cicada can be identified by the yellow spots on its back. Population levels fluctuate from year to year, and during certain years exceedingly large numbers can be found, leading many to confuse this species with periodical cicadas of the genus *Magicicada* (page 210). Males tend to call for long periods from stationary perches in trees, where they are approached by females ready to mate.

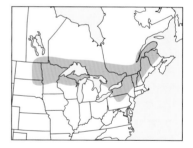

Song: An extended, cricketlike trill given at a rate of around 22 pulses per second. The peak frequency is about 9 kHz.

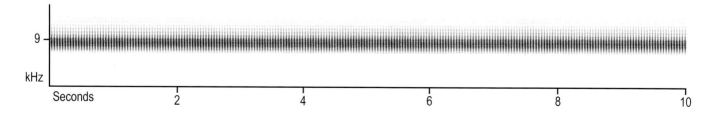

Common in northern deciduous forest habitats, the Say's Cicada is similar in appearance to the Canadian Cicada but can be recognized by its bright orange markings, especially on the underside of the abdomen, and also by its slightly larger body. Say's Cicada is semiperiodical, meaning it exhibits a strict four-year life cycle, but individuals can be found emerging in all years throughout its range. It is named after Thomas Say (1787–1834), the father of American entomology. The pupal shells have dark bands around the abdominal segments (see photo below).

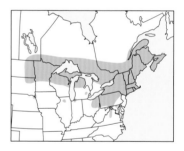

Song: A prolonged, high-pitched, metallic buzz with about 75 pulses per second at a frequency of 10 kHz. Sounds higher in pitch than the Canadian Cicada's song, probably because of its more rapid pulse rate. Say's Cicadas also give short songs, sometimes in a series. Short songs last two to three seconds and increase in loudness from beginning to end.

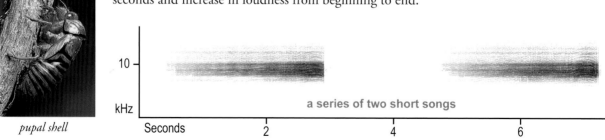

pupal shell

a series of two short songs

10 —

kHz

Seconds   2   4   6

With a vibrant turquoise and black forebody set against a pale golden abdomen, the delicate Hieroglyphic Cicada looks as if it is from a different world. Less than an inch long, it is predominantly southeastern in distribution and is often found in loose colonies in dry woods of oak and pine. Males typically sing from high perches and are difficult to capture, but sometimes they breed in young stands, where they perch on the bark of small trees. An early-season singer, it is heard from June through July.

Song: A high-pitched dissonant drone given all day long, reminiscent of the sound made by a model airplane. Songs typically last fifteen to twenty seconds and are often given one after the other. Songs start soft but quickly build in volume. There are usually distinct pulsations of loudness at the beginning, before the song becomes smooth and then tapers off at the end: *zeea-zeea-zeea-zeea-zeeeeeeeeeeeee* (some songs are mostly smooth throughout). There are two distinct peak frequencies, one at 5 kHz, the other at 10 kHz.

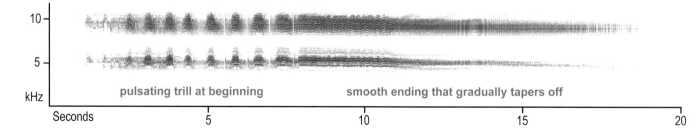

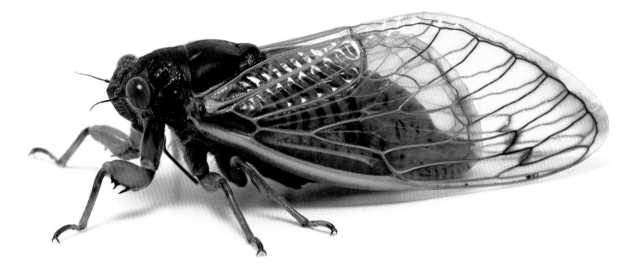

There are seven species of cicada in eastern North America that belong to the genus *Magicicada*—four species with thirteen-year life cycles and three with seventeen-year cycles. The seventeen-year species are generally northern in distribution, while the thirteen-year species are more southern and midwestern. In all species, individuals are so synchronized developmentally that they are nearly absent as adults in the twelve or sixteen years between emergences. When they do emerge after their long juvenile periods, they do so in huge numbers, forming dense aggregations. Entomologists often use the common name "periodical cicada" to refer to this genus alone. Periodical cicadas are often referred to as "17-year locusts" or "13-year locusts," but they are not actually locusts, which are short-horned grasshoppers in the order Orthoptera (page 178).

Magicicada adults have black bodies, striking red eyes, and orange legs and wing veins. Adults emerge in May or June and live for only a few weeks. Although nearly all of the periodical cicadas in a given region emerge the same year, cicadas in other regions may emerge in different years. All periodical cicadas of the same life-cycle type that emerge in a given year are collectively known as a "brood" or "year-class." See page 212 for the twelve brood maps of Linnaeus's 17-year Cicada, *Magicicada septendecim,* the species being featured here and one of the most well-known cicadas found in the eastern United States.

Song: Over the course of an emergence, male periodical cicadas congregate in huge choruses or singing aggregations, usually located high in trees. Fe-

pupal shell

female laying eggs in stem

males visit these aggregations and mate there. Males of all species have typical calling songs as well as special courtship songs, the latter being given only in the presence of females. In *Magicicada septendecim,* the calling song is a prolonged buzz that drops in pitch at the end: *weeeeeee-ah.* This song is very low-pitched, around 1.3 kHz, much lower than the calls of our other cicadas. When the male approaches a female, she responds by clicking her wings after each song, and he slurs his songs together. Finally, when he mounts the female, he gives a series of distinct staccato buzzes. The sonagram below depicts the male's typical calling song.

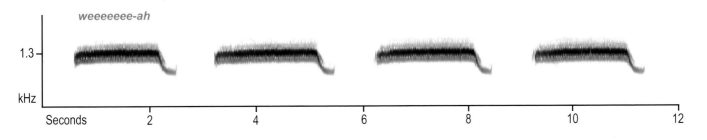

weeeeeeee-ah

1.3 -

kHz

Seconds   2   4   6   8   10   12

Linnaeus's 17-year Cicada Brood Maps—*Magicicada septendecim*

Brood I

1978, 1995, 2012, 2029

VA, WV

Brood V

1982, 1999, 2016, 2033

MD, OH, PA, VA, WV

Brood IX

1986, 2003, 2020, 2037

NC, VA, WV

Brood II

1979, 1996, 2013, 2030

CT, MD, NC, NJ, NY, PA, VA

Brood VI

1983, 2000, 2017, 2034

GA, NC, SC

Brood X

1987, 2004, 2021, 2038

DE, GA, IL, IN, KY, MD, MI, NC, NJ, NY, OH, PA, TN, VA, WV

Brood III

1980, 1997, 2014, 2031

IA, IL, MO

Brood VII

1984, 2001, 2018, 2035

NY

Brood XIII

1990, 2007, 2024, 2041

IA, IL, IN, MI, WI

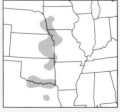

Brood IV

1981, 1998, 2015, 2032

IA, KS, MO, NB, OK, TX

Brood VIII

1985, 2002, 2019, 2036

OH, PA, WV

Brood XIV

1991, 2008, 2025, 2042

KY, GA, IN, MA, MD, NC, NJ, NY, OH, PA, TN, VA, WV

Note: The above twelve broods, designated by Roman numerals reflecting years in relation to Brood I, are the only broods documented for 17-year cicadas. Some years no 17-year cicadas emerge. These maps have been redrawn from maps found on the University of Michigan periodical cicada Web site, www.ummz.lsa.umich.edu/magicicada/Periodical/Index.html.

mating pair

Finding, Collecting, and Keeping Insects

To many, the late summer chorus of insects is experienced as disembodied sound—a plethora of trills, scrapes, shuffles, buzzes, ticks, and chirps that spring like magic from grass, shrubs, and trees. With few exceptions, the insect musicians themselves are difficult to find. Many are small and well camouflaged in their green and brown coats, and they sit motionless when they sing, blending into their surroundings. Some hide under or behind things, and many sing only in the dark of the night. So how does one find them? How does one catch a glimpse of the singers that are producing these wondrous sounds?

Finding singing insects is both challenging and fun. The majority have high-pitched songs, so good hearing is a necessity (see page 27). And sharp eyes are an asset, aided by flashlights when you're hunting at night. The first step is to home in on the general area in which an insect is singing. Tilt your head from side to side if you're confused about where the sound is coming from, and cup your ears when you do this, for more precise directionality. A slow and careful approach is also advised, because many insects will jump or hop away when disturbed, or else quit singing and move to the back of a stem or leaf. Move toward the singer while spiraling around his perch, or else try to triangulate his exact location by pointing at him from one position, then moving off to the side and pointing at him again—the insect is located where the two directional lines intersect. Triangulation is particularly useful at night. Two people can approach a singer from different directions. If both shine their flashlights at him at the same time, the insect will be located where the two light beams cross.

These techniques work well with insects that sing from grasses, weeds, and shrubs. But finding arboreal species is another matter. Sometimes, males can be found singing on low branches. And for those that sing from small trees, you can lay out a sheet below a tree and shake the tree vigorously, in the hope that the singer will fall to the ground. Look around after severe rainstorms that may have knocked individuals from their perches. In addition, many arboreal species are attracted to lights at night, and they may show up on your front porch, on window screens, or around illuminated food and beverage vendor machines.

Once you locate a singer, what are you going to do with it? You might only want to watch it. If you sit quietly and wait, many species will relax and begin singing, so that you can observe the singing posture and especially the movement of the wings. You might also want to collect a singer, so that you can get a closer look and perhaps take him home for further observation. Using a container with a tight-fitting lid, you can maneuver the opening toward the insect, with the lid positioned on the opposite side. Then, with a quick motion, close the container around your quarry, perhaps including a little vegetation. Many singers can actually be enticed to jump right into the container. Be careful not to injure the insect or accidentally pin him between the lid and the container. Other techniques are also useful, such as sweeping through grass or weeds with an insect net.

Most entomologists agree that insect populations are unaffected by small-scale collecting, so you may want to catch males of several different species and transport them home to create a personal "orchestra of insect musi-

Sword-bearing Conehead — cool to look at but too loud for the home

cians" that will fill your home with their songs. You can transfer captured insects to simple screen cages that look nice in a household setting. Cicadas should not be kept as pets because most die quickly in captivity, but most crickets and katydids adapt well and seem to thrive on a simple diet of iceberg lettuce.

If you bring singing insects into your home, be sure to choose species with songs that appeal to you. Crickets with delicate trills and chirps are quite pleasing to the ear, as are the high-pitched shuffles and ticks of various meadow katydids. While the Common True Katydid sings too harshly to keep as a pet, many of the false katydids have pleasing and intermittent songs. The coneheads are to be avoided. While their appearance is interesting, their songs are generally loud and harsh and will drown out the other instruments in your insect orchestra.

For a list of species that make good pets, along with instructions for building an attractive cage and tips concerning the proper care of captive insect singers, visit our Web site, www.songsofinsects.com.

The Photographs and Sound Recordings

PHOTOGRAPHS

Virtually all the photographs in this book were taken by the authors, with only a few exceptions (see list on the facing page). When we earnestly began fieldwork for the book in 2000 (preliminary work on the book actually dates back to the mid-1990s), we were both using color slide film. During our expeditions across eastern North America, we would take lots of photos and then head to nearby cities in order to get the slides developed, so that we could judge our success before moving to a new location. All that changed, of course, with the digital revolution. By 2004 we were racing down the homestretch working purely in the digital domain, and around half the photos in this book are from digital cameras.

Our most recent equipment list included Canon 1Ds Mark II and Canon 1Ds digital camera bodies. Our favorite lens was the Canon 180mm f/3.5 Macro, which we sometimes used in conjuction with the Canon 1.4x or 2x teleconverters. Nearly all photographs were supplemented by electronic flash, using various Canon Speedlights. We often utilized a tripod with a ball head, but the short duration of electronic flashes allowed many photos to be taken handheld.

Two kinds of photographs are featured in this book. The ones showing insects on vegetation either were taken directly in the field or were made indoors where we had more control over the situation. When we collected an insect for photography, we would also collect samples of the vegetation upon which it was found, allowing us to reconstruct a natural setup at home or in a motel.

Swamp Cicada

The second type of photographs featured are the striking pictures of the insects on a white surface. We accomplished this by constructing a special "whitebox" out of artist foam board. The slanted top of the whitebox was covered with clouded Plexiglas, which dispersed bright light from electronic flashes in order to produce subtle shadows. Each insect was placed inside the box on a white disk that could be easily rotated. In those rare instances when the specimen would pause in an acceptable posture, we would carefully rotate the disk to optimize the angle and then take pictures until the insect started moving again. Visit www.songsofinsects.com for photos of our whitebox setup.

The following is a list of the five photographs taken by people other than the authors.

Thomas J. Walker
    page 58, Four-spotted Tree Cricket, singing
        from a hole in a leaf
    page 158, Fork-tailed Bush Katydid, pink
        color morph (female)

Mari Maloney-Watkins
    page 142, Rattler Round-winged Katydid,
        rare pink color morph

P. Allen Woodliffe
    page 148, Oblong-winged Katydid, pink
        and yellow color morphs

Kathy Hill
    page 203, Robinson's Cicada, green form

SOUND RECORDINGS

All the sound recordings on the compact disc were made by the authors, with only one exception: the Southern Mole Cricket, recorded by Thomas J. Walker. We used Sony TCD-D10 ProII digital audio tape recorders equipped with SoundDevices MP-3 outboard preamps. Recordings were made both in the field and in the lab, mostly using Sennheiser MKH60 shotgun microphones. In addition, we used various parabolic microphone set-ups in those instances when we could not get close to the singers, such as with cicadas and certain tree crickets that sound off from high in trees. We also collected numerous stereo recordings of insect choruses or soundscapes that we used to create our supplementary *Insect Concertos* disc, described on page 221.

Our digital recordings were transferred to computer hard drives and preliminary editing was done on both Macs and PCs using digital sound-editing programs. The final assembly of the recordings was accomplished using Adobe Audition software.

Fall Field Cricket

Sources and Further Reading

We consulted many sources in the creation of this work and cannot include them all here. Below are listed some of the most important, including recent books, some older historical works we found useful, a comprehensive new Web site featuring insect songs, and two previous audio guides. Please also visit our support Web site, www.songsofinsects.com.

Recent Books

John L. Capinera, Ralph D. Scott, and Thomas J. Walker. 2004. *Field Guide to Grasshoppers, Katydids, and Crickets of the United States.* Ithaca: Cornell University Press. 249 pages. An up-to-date field guide and reference work that includes range maps, natural history information, sonagrams, and drawings of museum specimens.

Darryl T. Gwynne. 2001. *Katydids and Bush-Crickets: Reproductive Behavior and Evolution of the Tettigoniidae.* Ithaca: Comstock Publishing. 317 pages. A synthesis of the natural history of the katydids with a critical eye to the scientific literature.

Lisa Gail Ryan. 1996. *Insect Musicians and Cricket Champions: A Cultural History of Singing Insects in China and Japan.* San Francisco: China Books and Periodicals, Inc. A delightful treatise on the cultural history of singing insects in China and Japan, with photos of insect cages, Oriental drawings of crickets and katydids, and reprints of two classic essays on insect musicians.

Vincent Dethier. 1992. *Crickets and Katydids, Concerts and Solos.* Cambridge: Harvard University Press. 140 pages. A compelling, personal account by Dr. Dethier of his summers as an undergraduate in the late 1930s collecting singing insects for Dr. George W. Pierce, at Pierce's field station in New Hampshire.

Franz Huber, Thomas Moore, and Werner Loher. 1989. *Cricket Behavior and Neurobiology.* Ithaca: Comstock Publishing. 565 pages. An introduction to cricket acoustic behavior and neurobiology. A very complete reference.

Vernon R. Vickery and D. Keith McE. Kevan. 1985. *The Insects and Arachnids of Canada, Part 14: The Grasshoppers, Crickets, and Related Insects of Canada and Adjacent Regions.* Ottawa: Canada Communication Group. 918 pages. A technical guide to Canadian Orthopterans, including range maps and natural history information.

Some Older Books and Articles

Richard D. Alexander, A. E. Pace, and Daniel Otte. 1972. "The Singing Insects of Michigan." *Great Lakes Entomologist*, 5: 33–69.

Richard D. Alexander. 1960. "Sound Communication in Orthoptera and Cicadidae." In *Animal Sounds and Communication*, 7: 38–92. American Institute of Biological Science Publications.

George W. Pierce. 1948. *The Songs of Insects, with Related Material on the Production, Propagation, Detection, and Measurement of Supersonic Vibrations.* Cambridge: Harvard University Press. 329 pages. A classic scientific work on insect sounds, documenting Dr. Pierce's pioneering research into the physics of sound production in insects.

Willis S. Blatchley. 1920. *Orthoptera of Northeastern America with Especial Reference to the Fauna of Indiana and Florida.* Indianapolis: Nature Publishing Company. 784 pages. A valuable early technical treatment.

A. P. Morse. 1920. "Manual of the Orthoptera of New England." *Proceedings of the Boston Society of Natural History,* 35: 197–556.

Samuel H. Scudder. 1892. *The Songs of Our Grasshoppers and Crickets.* Annual Report of the Entomological Society of Ontario, 22: 62–78.

Charles H. Fernald. 1888. *The Orthopera of New England.* Boston: Wright & Potter.

Tom Walker's Web Site

Thomas J. Walker, an entomologist at the University of Florida, has created Singing Insects of North America, a Web site featuring crickets and katydids (a colleague, Dr. Thomas E. Moore, is in the process of adding cicadas to the site). Features hundreds of sound recordings along with detailed scientific references. We highly recommend this Web site: www.buzz.ifas.ufl.edu.

Audio Guides

Surprisingly, there have been only two audio guides to insect sounds published in North America prior to this book-and-disc:

Steve Rannels, Wil Hershberger, and Joseph Dillon. 1998. *The Songs of Crickets and Katydids of the Mid-Atlantic States* (audio compact disc). A regional audio guide to the songs of forty-three species. Self-published. Can be ordered from this book's Web site: www.songsofinsects.com.

Donald J. Borror and Richard D. Alexander. 1956. *The Songs of Insects: Calls of the Common Crickets, Grasshoppers, and Cicadas of Eastern United States.* Borror Laboratory of Bioacoustics, Ohio State University. A classic phonodisc guide to the songs of forty species, now available on compact disc from the Borror Laboratory's Web site: www.blb.biosci.ohio-state.edu.

Snowy Tree Cricket

Singing Insect Note Cards

The insects in this book look wonderful when photographed against white, so we've created the Singing Insect Note Card Series, which features a number of the most outstanding species. On the backs of the cards are descriptions of the songs, along with a Web page address where the songs can actually be heard. To learn all about this unique note card series, visit www.songsofinsects.com.

Relax to the Songs of Insects

In late summer and early autumn, the gently throbbing choruses of insects relax the spirit and soothe the mind. So that you can experience these insect lullabies during all months of the year, we have created *Insect Concertos,* our first compact disc in what we hope will be a growing series. Featuring stereo soundscapes that convey the natural mix of sounds, this CD does not contain any narration — only the pure, unadulterated songs of our native crickets, katydids, and cicadas. To learn more about this CD, visit www.songsofinsects.com.

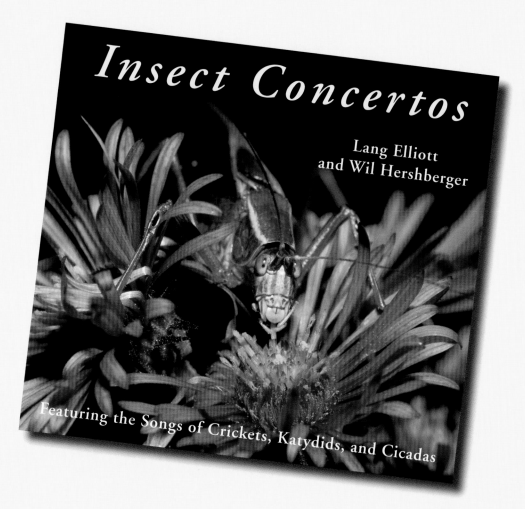

Acknowledgments

Many people have contributed to the creation of this book, and we offer sincere thanks to all who have supported and encouraged us along the way, including family and friends and the following individuals.

• Tom Walker, for his extensive research on singing insects. Tom acted as our principal scientific advisor and content editor. His encyclopedic singing insect Web site, which includes sound recordings and range maps, was the primary source of the natural history information summarized in this book.

• Vincent Dethier, biologist extraordinaire, for his poetic genius, and for inspiring the creation of this guide.

• Donna Hershberger, for keeping insects alive while we were in the field and for unfailing personal support throughout the long-drawn-out process.

• Catherine Landis, kindred spirit and *Scudderia* aficionado with an inborn appreciation of insect song; we thank you for being your enthusiastic, supportive self.

• Sarah Padula, for help with collecting katydids and for selflessly providing a home for a full orchestra of noisy insects—a guest room temporarily converted to a lab where many of the recordings and photographs in this book were made.

• John Zyla, for helping us construct cicada range maps, sending us specimens, and helping us track down *Neocicada hieroglyphica*.

• Cicada researchers Dave Marshall, Kathy Hill, and John Cooley, for providing the opportunity to record and photograph 17-year cicadas at their North Carolina study site, for helping us find *Okanagana* specimens in northern Michigan, and for invaluable editing of the cicada section text.

• Les Daniels, cicada enthusiast from Ohio, for providing much-needed *Tibicen* specimens.

• Sam Droege of Patuxent Wildlife Research, for arranging a visit to Irish Grove on the Eastern Shore of Maryland, where we recorded a number of new species.

• Lisa White and Anne Chalmers of Houghton Mifflin Company, for expert editing and for helping us refine the design of the book.

And last but not least, we applaud the insects themselves, who have given us the opportunity to celebrate the beauty of their songs. Thank you, insect musicians, one and all, for filling our lives with your melodies.

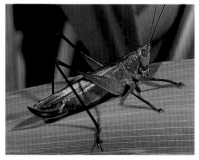

Black-legged Meadow Katydid (female)

Index to Species and Groups

This index refers to page numbers and includes both common and scientific names along with major groups. Boldface page numbers indicate species photos. Refer to the "Species List" on pages 31–32 for a list of species arranged by taxonomic groups and keyed to species numbers that are coordinated with the compact disc. The contents on page 7 should be used as a general subject index.

Handsome Meadow Katydid

Broad-winged Bush Katydid